To Anita & Lind
warmest

dare to believe

# dare to believe

explore your own
psychic abilities with TV medium

## jeanette wilson

RANDOM HOUSE
NEW ZEALAND

National Library of New Zealand Cataloguing-in-Publication Data
Wilson, Jeanette, 1962-
Dare to believe / Jeanette Wilson.
ISBN-13: 978-1-86941-768-0
ISBN-10: 1-86941-768-2
1. Psychic ability. 2. Spiritualism. I. Title.
133.91—dc 22


A RANDOM HOUSE BOOK
published by
Random House New Zealand
18 Poland Road, Glenfield, Auckland, New Zealand
www.randomhouse.co.nz

First published 2006

© 2006 Jeanette Wilson

The moral rights of the author have been asserted

ISBN-13: 978 1 86941 768 0
ISBN-10: 1 86941 768 2

Design: Sharon Grace
Cover design: Katy Yiakmis
Cover photograph: Chris Coad
Pendulum illustration: Deb Hinde
Printed in Australia by Griffin Press

# CONTENTS

Prelude     7

**Part 1: DARE TO BELIEVE ...**
that there is a different way to look at this world and your place in it

Chapter 1 — The door     19
Chapter 2 — The map     33

**Part 2: DARE TO BELIEVE ...**
that you are more than you yet perceive yourself to be

Chapter 3 — Know yourself     51
Chapter 4 — New eyes     71
Chapter 5 — Finding your truth     96

**Part 3: DARE TO BELIEVE ...**
that you have abilities that you have not yet discovered

Chapter 6 — Receiving guidance     117
Chapter 7 — Relaxation, visualisation and meditation     136
Chapter 8 — Guides     153
Chapter 9 — Connecting with your Higher Self     168
Chapter 10 — Mediumship     178

**Part 4: DARE TO BELIEVE ...**
that you really can make a difference

Chapter 11 — Dare to be you     193

# PRELUDE

Imagine being able to see and talk to loved ones who have passed over whenever you wanted to. Imagine being able to say all the things you still needed to say to them, and how that would help you move through your own emotions.

Imagine how you would feel *knowing* that your loved ones, whom you thought had died, had not really 'died' at all. Even better, imagine having the ability to sense them with you at important and difficult times, when you needed them.

Have you ever wondered what it would be like to be able to see that relative you never knew, and get to know him or her? Or what it would be like to receive guidance from your higher-level guides, whenever and however you needed it?

Difficult life situations are infinitely easier to work through when you know what is really going on, what your real choices are and what lessons they are teaching you.

Imagine how it would feel knowing why you are here, and why the people around you are in your life. Wouldn't it make for an easier, more peaceful life? If we understand *why* we are having an experience it often helps us to be more tolerant towards it.

My journey to becoming a medium is detailed in my first

book, *Medium Rare*. My experiences as a medium are detailed in my second book, *Rare Moments*. In both of my previous books I share stories with you from my journey, because stories help us to learn. We don't all have to go through the same experiences; if we can heed someone else's lessons we may not have to walk that path ourselves. I also share insights I have received along my own particular journey, and conclusions I have reached.

Both my previous books have helped pave the way for this one. In this book, *Dare to Believe*, I share with you more of the *process* I went through to get to who/how I now am, and how that process played a significant part in developing my abilities.

No matter where you are starting from, there will be value for you in this book. The tools it offers can be used over and over again to help you progress further along your own individual path.

From the very beginning, for reasons I didn't then understand, I was guided not to read about anyone else's experiences of mediumship and not to go to the Spiritualist Church (which is where you would normally go to develop such abilities). It wasn't that there was anything wrong with the Spiritualist Church; it was just that, for the work I was here to do, I needed to have my *own* pure experiences, not influenced by anyone else's ideas, interpretations, or limitations.

And so I taught myself how to find the answers I needed, and how to talk to beings/aspects of consciousness from the different dimensions at will. It was a hard path at times and quite lonely until I met my life partner, Andrew. I don't think it was by chance that Andrew had also had to walk a path of finding his own answers for many years before he met me. If people lean on each other too much for the answers they often find that when those people are not around they have a tendency to topple over. We each need to find our own way; a way that works for us.

At times the temptation to seek the easy way out, to find an answer in a book or through another person, was quite strong but, in the long run, finding the answers for myself has paid off immeasurably. I learned not only to 'receive' my own guidance when I needed it and in a way that I could understand, but I also learned the *mechanics* of how to receive guidance and talk to beings in the different dimensions.

In 2005 my television series *Dare to Believe* launched in New Zealand, and it became apparent that there were far more people needing to see me than I could ever possibly meet. Each night that the television show went to air there would be more than 3,000 visits to my website. We had to take the contact details off the website because we just couldn't cope with the number of enquiries we were receiving.

I realised that many of the people felt that they needed to see me, to talk to me, to talk with their loved ones, to ask questions, or just to find out more. I also realised that many of these people wouldn't really need to see me at all if they were able to access their own guidance and talk to their own loved ones. So that is what a lot of this book is about. It is designed to help *you* receive your own higher guidance and to talk with your own loved ones at will.

Looking back, it seems glaringly obvious that the timing

of my first encounter with the spirit world was very well thought through at some level. I believe it was more than coincidence that at the time I first discovered that I had abilities as a medium, I was training in something called NLP (Neuro Linguistic Programming). NLP is at the forefront of the psychological tools that can help us better understand ourselves and tap into our unlimited potential. I soon grasped that, by using NLP tools, I would be able to accelerate my learning as a medium by being exquisitely conscious of what was happening within me as I communicated with either my own guides or loved ones who had passed over.

I spent considerable time developing my abilities to the highest possible standard, both in the UK, my original home, and then in New Zealand, my current home, before demonstrating mediumship to large audiences for the first time.

It also seems significant that, before discovering my abilities as a medium, I worked as a professional trainer for Lloyds Bank for several years. This experience in personal development has proved invaluable in many ways. It has helped me to break down quite complex ideas into bite-sized chunks that I and others can understand, and it has also helped me to understand *how* people learn. The following diagram shows how people learn, and keep on learning.

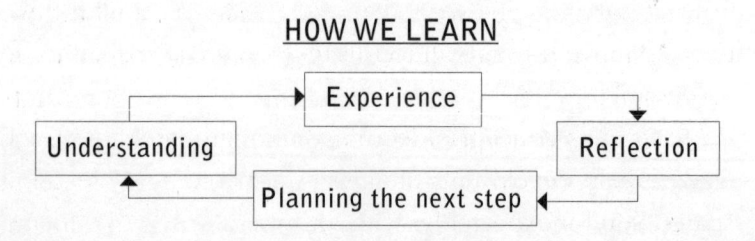

## HOW WE LEARN

Experience → Reflection → Planning the next step → Understanding → Experience

PRELUDE

Generally, when we learn to do something new we pass through each of these stages in turn. Say, for example, you want to learn to ride a bike. As a child, many of us would just have got on it, held the handle bars and had a go at pedalling while our parents held us upright. We would start with an *experience*.

If we fell off we would rub our head or our knees, and *reflect* on what had happened, perhaps replaying it in our mind's eye. We would want to *understand* why we fell off — perhaps we braked too hard or hit the kerb. Then, using that knowledge, we would *plan* what to do differently next time, and we would have climbed back on the bike for another *experience*.

But some children don't do that; they fall off and hurt themselves and then do exactly the same again. Others fall off and don't get back on, at least not for some time. Their learning, and their growth, is limited by not moving on to the other stages of learning.

To learn effectively we need to move through *all* the stages of learning. The time it takes to do that is different for each of us, and depends on what it is we are learning.

One thing that is constant though is the *process*, whether we are talking about a child riding a bike or an adult learning how to manage a life situation or talk to the spirit world. We need to move through all four stages in turn if we are to be successful.

It was this concept of learning, among others, that I first used to help develop my abilities as a medium. My learning started very unexpectedly, with an *experience*. At 31, for no apparent reason and without prior warning, I could suddenly see and hear spirit beings as clearly as I could a living person. At first I didn't know what was happening to me. It was only when I *reflected* on what had happened, and on the preceding events, that I was slowly able to piece things together. Then I wanted to *understand why and how* it had happened. Would it happen again or was it a one-off event? It was only with time and understanding that I was able to draw some conclusions about what had happened. Initially, they were very tentative conclusions that I would need to test out.

It was those tentative conclusions that helped me to identify and *plan my next steps*. I was not sure if what had happened to me had happened just to wake me up spiritually, or if it was a sign that I was a medium. There was only one way to find out. I needed to put myself to the test and find out whether I really could talk to loved ones who had passed over. In other words, I needed more *experience*.

Fortunately, there was no shortage of people happy for me to practise my skill on. I started with my immediate family, then with friends as I became more confident. At each stage I asked for feedback on the messages and information that came through me. My 'research' was taking up a lot of my spare time, and I didn't want to be deluding myself, let alone anyone else, that I had such an ability.

It soon became clear that I really was able to talk to the spirit world, because there was no way I could possibly have known the details that were conveyed through me. Mathematically, the odds of me getting the information correct would have been millions to one.

As time went on, I asked for more and more specific feedback to help me to identify what information was accurate and what wasn't. I wanted to be sure which information came from 'spirit' and which was either wishful thinking or my imagination. Using the NLP tools I had already learned, I was able to observe my own eye movements, and those of other mediums, to understand what was happening within me when I 'received' information.

I was also able to observe my own internal processes and to note where in my being I was holding my consciousness when I made a successful link with either a loved one or a guide. When I *reflected* on my experiences I knew that, with NLP and with what I knew about *how* I learned, I had all the tools I needed to get mediumship down to a fine art.

I was learning quickly what worked and what didn't. But, more importantly, I was starting to understand why. That in turn led me to devise and plan more experiments or experiences. On and on I went through the different stages of learning, developing and refining my abilities as I went. When I got 'stuck' I found it was almost always because I had allowed myself to stay in one of the stages of learning too long — just like the child who is too afraid to get back onto the bike.

The knowledge of this learning process has served me well, and not only with mediumship. I have applied it in many areas of my life. What fascinates me is that most children and adults I have shown this process to tell me that, until seeing the stages, they were not really aware of *how* they learned. They recognised that there had been times when they learned something easily and times when they hadn't found it so easy. Just seeing this process written down helped them to understand *how* they could learn better. So, just by being aware of *how* you learn, being *conscious* of it, you start to accelerate your learning and your own personal growth.

There are many opportunities for you to accelerate your own learning as you read through this book. I will invite you to have new experiences, and to reflect on these experiences. I will encourage you to develop new understandings, to consider your experiences in the light of these new understandings, and then to plan your next steps in a way that is comfortable for you.

It is worth mentioning that, as you work through this book, you may find that you have a natural preference for one or more of the learning stages. Just by reading this introduction you may have already recognised where you would feel most comfortable. However, for maximum growth and learning you need to spend time in *each* of the stages. If you find yourself skipping the same stages again and again, perhaps you need to look at *why* that is and what you may be missing out on.

As in life, it doesn't matter which of the four learning stages we start with. In some chapters of this book we may start with an experience and in others we may start by reflecting about what has happened in the past, or by introducing a new understanding. As long as you go through all four stages in turn you will still find that you maximise your learning.

But this book isn't just about learning how to be a medium or how to develop psychic abilities. The main purpose is to open your eyes to who you truly are. It is only by understanding the true nature of your being that you can uncover just what is possible here in this physical reality, and the abilities that you do not yet know you have.

But, to move from the place you are currently at, you need to be willing to open your mind further than it has been opened before.

---

**Dare you believe** that there is a different way to look at this world and your place in it?
**Dare you believe** that you are more than you yet perceive yourself to be?
**Dare you believe** that you have abilities you have not yet discovered?
**Dare you believe** that you really can make a difference?!

And I have to warn you: if you do start to explore any of these areas, there will be no going back. When you start to see things differently, your life begins to change. You can't go back to your old way of seeing the world or your old way of being, any more than I could go back to being a bank manager.

Your life will change in profound and unexpected ways. In fact, only one thing is assured — your life will never be the same again.

Are you ready?

# PART 1

# DARE TO BELIEVE...

that there is a different way to look at this world and your place in it

## CHAPTER 1

# THE DOOR

> The most beautiful thing we can experience is the mysterious. It is the source of all true art and science.
>
> — ALBERT EINSTEIN

The woman on stage with me was distraught, the most upset I had ever seen someone at one of my shows. She had turned her chair away from the audience so they could not see her distress. She was bent over, her shoulders heaving as she cried seemingly unstoppable tears.

Part of me was panicking inside; it was awful to see her like this. This wasn't what the message from her late husband was supposed to do. I didn't know what to do or what to say. I needed some help with how to handle this situation and I needed it quickly.

Usually I am warned in advance if a message is likely to be too emotional to convey on stage, and I see the person privately after the show. But this time it seemed I was caught out. Quickly I handed the lady a clutch of tissues and internally I pleaded with her husband Tony, in spirit, for something that would help her.

Tony, her husband who had passed over quite recently, was with me strongly. I could feel him in my physical body, above me and to my left. Physically, he had been quite a bit bigger than me. His presence was clear and his demeanour remained surprisingly calm and matter of fact, despite his wife's obvious distress.

Tony said to ask her about his shoes. I felt my heart sink. How on earth would asking about something as trivial as his shoes help? I despaired, but was at a loss for what to do or say. I found the words Tony had suggested coming out of my mouth.

'Do you still have his shoes?' I asked tentatively. The reaction was as immediate as it was surprising. The tears stopped as abruptly as they had started. I didn't understand why, but for some reason my question about Tony's shoes had clearly stopped her emotions in their tracks. Her head came up and she looked at me out of the corner of a tear-filled eye. She was holding a crumpled tissue close to her face, clutching it tightly in her hand; her face was bright red from all the tears and emotion. Her husband in spirit was laughing about his shoes in my head. How could he be like this when she was so upset? I was cross with him, and frustrated that I still didn't understand why asking about his shoes should be so significant.

'Why is he laughing about his shoes?' I continued curiously, wondering why on earth Tony would choose to talk about his shoes when there must be so many other more meaningful things to say.

'It is rather odd I suppose,' she said, wiping away her tears.

Her face was starting to brighten and I noticed there was the beginning of a smile.

'What have you done with them?' I gently prompted as I returned her smile.

The audience was spellbound; it was as though no one dared breathe. All the audience's attention was focused on what had happened to her late husband's shoes.

'I have planted flowers in them' she said laughing. All at once she could see the funny side of how that must sound. It wasn't everyone who planted flowers in their late partner's shoes!

The audience collapsed into laughter and I did too. The almost unbearable tension had been broken. Her face was brighter, her eyes were clear, and all the pain of a few moments before had simply dissolved. Tony had found exactly the right thing to say to show her it really was him, that he knew about the shoes and that he really was still with her. In the process he had put a smile on her face — something that had seemed impossible just moments before. He clearly knew her well, and his timing had been impeccable. I could feel myself relaxing as she smiled back at me.

The audience's laughter barely had time to subside before I watched her smile turn into a frown. I held my breath as she looked directly at me. I could see the tears welling in her eyes once more, and I was half expecting the dam to burst again. All the pain and the hurt were back. 'He promised he would get through to me. Why hasn't he?' There was desperation in her voice as it trailed to a whisper.

I didn't know the answer. I didn't know why he hadn't

got through to her. I put my own feelings to one side and let my awareness focus internally once more with Tony's spirit. I asked him quite forcefully why he hadn't got through to her when he promised he would. I wanted to know too — why hadn't he, when he could see she was in this much pain?

The audience was silent as I waited for a response. It took a moment or two. You could have heard a pin drop, and it crossed my mind that the entire audience wanted to know the answer to this one too.

'Because the door opens from your side' was his straightforward reply when it came. Tony had found that the door opened from this side, meaning the physical dimension. It is up to us in the physical dimension to open the door and so facilitate contact with our loved ones in the other dimensions.

I wondered how many other grieving widows, widowers, mothers, fathers, brothers, sisters and even children waited for their loved ones to come through as they had promised and, when they didn't, gave up hope of there being an afterlife. Certainly, from my own experience, it had been 31 years before I had any indication that the spirit world even existed, and I had come across so many people, like the woman on stage with me, who were desperate to know that their loved ones were alright.

It wasn't until later that evening that I was able to reflect more fully on the significance of Tony's message. At virtually every show there is something new for me to learn. It may be about how to communicate with a particular loved one, how to deal with a particular kind of audience, or how to learn what a particular symbol means. More usually it is some kind of information that is 'new' to me, some kind of insight.

Tony's message about the door opening from this side was new to me but, on refection, it also made perfect sense. The 'door' opens from this side. I knew this was profoundly significant. At the time I wasn't sure how I had opened the door 10 years earlier at the NLP workshop, but somehow I had. A whole new world had opened up to me — one where I could see and talk to beings in the other dimensions at will.

What if I could work out how I had managed to open that door? What if that knowledge could help others to open up the door? People would not need to experience the same amount of pain as the woman who had been on stage with me. Instead, they would be able to talk to their loved ones at will. They would still miss their physical presence, but their pain would be less knowing that they would meet up with them again on the other side of life.

They would also be able to receive guidance from their loved ones and their guides about their life situation and the choices they faced. Perhaps this awareness of their loved ones in the spiritual dimensions could even help people release their own fear of death, so making their own passing more peaceful when the time came.

The potential benefits were clearly enormous and I couldn't help wondering if this was why, before being awakened psychically, I had been given the opportunity to learn to be a professional trainer. It was looking very much as though part of my role was to help others to open that door.

I realised it was time to start sharing, not only the content of what had happened to me over the last 10 years, but also to share more of the process of how to open that door. This book is not though *just* about developing psychically. It is also about developing the whole you and expanding your perception of reality. If you try to do the psychic development without an awareness of the bigger picture of who you are, you run the risk of getting out of balance.

As you go through the exercises in this book do them in sequence. Do not skip to the later exercises, as much as you may want to, until you have worked through the earlier ones. There is much more to psychic development than there first appears to be and it is important to have some knowledge of what you are doing — the mechanics if you like — to get the best results.

I first opened the door to the spirit world when I was on an NLP workshop. Before attending the workshop there had been only three experiences in my entire life that I could call 'psychic' in any way. The first was as a teenager, when I 'knew' that we were going to move house before my parents told me. I thought nothing of it at the time as I reasoned I must have somehow picked up clues from my parents. Another time I 'knew' I would have a maths test the next day — and I did. But again, I convinced myself I must have picked something up from my teacher, although no one else in the class had. The third incident was less easy to explain away.

On holiday in Cyprus and travelling in a taxi, I heard a man's voice tell me that the young man I had just met would 'look after me for a few years.' It was such a profound experience that I asked my friend, who was in the taxi with me, if she too had heard the voice. She hadn't, and no more was said about it. The young man did go on to look after me for a few years, exactly as the voice had said he would.

In each case I can still see in my mind's eye exactly where I was when I 'received' the information, which in itself is quite curious, but I had not linked the three occasions until I was asked about my previous psychic experiences by a reporter.

When I suddenly became able to see the spirit world on the NLP course my logical conclusion was that, somehow, something that I did on the course had caused me to tap into my *latent* abilities, abilities I had always had.

Have you ever known who was going to be on the end of a phone before you picked it up? Or that a particular bill or letter was going to arrive in the post? Have you ever thought of someone you had not seen in years and then bumped into them? All of these events, and others you may be able to think of, are evidence of a latent psychic ability.

I considered that, if such abilities were latent within me, perhaps it was reasonable to assume that others had similar abilities. Over the years I have put my theory to the test and have been fortunate to work with a great many people, individually and in groups, to explore psychic abilities.

I have found that many people have had similar experiences to my own, where they just *knew* something without any underlying reason or explanation, and that many have had experiences which they cannot explain. I have found that we all have abilities. It is just that some abilities are stronger in some people than in others and, as a general rule, you need to find your own natural strengths for the best results.

I found myself spending a lot of time thinking about the NLP workshop I had attended. Why did my abilities suddenly open up at that time? Was the workshop just a safe and friendly environment away from my normal more business-like workplace, or was there more to it?

The workshop was open to people from all walks of life. A large part of it was about finding out who we were or, rather, who we had chosen to be this lifetime, and unlocking our full potential. Some exercises were done individually, some in pairs and some in larger groups, so I found I was working with different people at different times. They were a friendly group and, with the trainer's help, I had relaxed in their company from day one, despite there being 64 participants, the largest workshop I had ever known.

It was strange though that no one else seemed to be having experiences anything like what was happening to me, yet we all went through the same exercises. Why had the other 63 participants not been affected in the same way? This was something that puzzled me a lot in the early days.

It is only in recent years that I have come to understand the significance of the events that led to that spiritual breakthrough. I realised that it was my choice of *what* I worked on at the workshop that accelerated the change in me and played a significant part in triggering my ability to see the spirit world. At the time, I wasn't able to put all the pieces of the jigsaw together but it became obvious that there was a clearly defined sequence of events which, with hindsight, even had an underlying logic to them.

It wasn't long before an interesting question arose within me — if the series of events and exercises I had experienced could affect me the way they had, could they affect others in the same way?

So I started to experiment, working with individuals and small groups to explore whether it really can be that simple. In this book I share with you the different exercises, and insights that I experienced at the NLP workshop, in more or less the order they happened. At times the journey may not seem logical, but bear with me. Sometimes it is clearer to see the path *after* you have walked it, just as it was for me.

On any journey, it is useful to know where you are starting from. At the start of the workshop, as a means of introducing ourselves to the rest of the group, we thought about who we currently were and how we were spending our lives. We collated our thoughts in writing and images in a format similar to the one below, developed by American NLP trainer Robert Dilts.

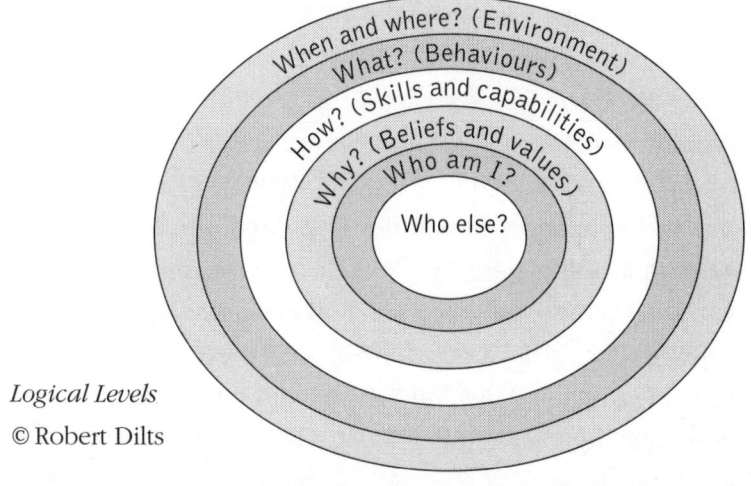

When and where? (Environment)
What? (Behaviours)
How? (Skills and capabilities)
Why? (Beliefs and values)
Who am I?
Who else?

*Logical Levels*
© Robert Dilts

We considered our *environment* — where and when we worked; our *behaviours* — what we did; our *skills and capabilities* — how we did what we did; and then our *beliefs and values*.

The outer rings became quite full very quickly, but as we got closer to the centre of the diagram I noticed people looking around for inspiration. Many of us, myself included, found it really difficult to answer the inner two questions: *Who am I?* and *Who else do I believe exists?* But after prompting by the trainer or one of his assistants, we eventually managed to put something in, even if it was 'I do not know' or a question-mark.

The rings were explained to us as a model — *a way of looking at why people behave the way they do*. I have found it helpful to think of this model as three-dimensional — a bit like those Russian dolls that fit one inside the other. We exist in an environment — in a certain community within a certain country at a certain point in time. Our interaction with our environment is shown predominantly by our behaviours — the next ring in — how we act or behave in our environment or with regard to others. In other words, *what* we do. Within that ring are our skills and capabilities — *How we do what we do*.

Let me give an example to help you understand the thinking behind the *Logical Levels* model more fully. For our behaviour to be polite and courteous (what we do) we would have had to have learned manners (acquired skills and capabilities) at some stage. We may have simply picked up good manners by observing the polite behaviour of others, such as brothers and sisters, or we may have had more formal training. The behaviours we display depend on the skills and capabilities that underlie them. These may be either natural or learned.

Our motivation to learn a particular skill or capability is determined by our beliefs and values — the next ring in (why we do what we do). For example, if we do not value or respect other people, we are unlikely to value learning manners. Simply giving a child more training about manners will not help them behave better if there is no underlying respect for other people, other people's property and the environment. However, if you teach a child to value other children, animals, property and their environment, their behaviours towards all of these will usually be influenced for the better, with minimal training and guidance.

I find the *Logical Levels* model useful to help me understand why people behave the way they do. In this book we will be using these levels to help us understand ourselves better. In this chapter we are exploring where we are starting from; later we will use them as a tool to help us recognise how we would prefer things to be.

In the following diagram you will find my *Logical Levels* for how I was when I attended the NLP workshop, and a copy for someone else, to show you how different, and yet similar, these models can be. After looking at these you will be asked to make your own copy. Use the questions from the first two examples as a prompt to help you complete it. It can be as basic or as comprehensive as you like.

## My example
**Where? When?**
I work mainly in Leeds but travel around the north. I live in Tadcaster, North Yorkshire. 1994.
**What?**
Training Manager for the North of England. I run workshops for managers and senior clerical staff.
I manage a team of six trainers, based in Manchester and Leeds.
Interests: Reading, psychology and NLP, home improvements.
**How?**
I hold an ACIB and a DipM.
I am a professional trainer.
I am trained in sales and sales marketing.
**Why?**
I like helping people to learn.
My new role enables me to be closer to my family.
**Who?**
?
**Who else?**
? I like to think that there is a greater power looking after us.

## Another example
**Where? When?**
Work is mainly in London though there is occasional overseas travel.
1995. Home is in Kent
**What?**

Fundraising manager for an international charity.
Marketing campaigns. Generating new ways to raise funds.
Managing a small team.
Visits to key areas overseas. Sharing of information within the organisation and across other charities.
Managing key relationships with corporate clients.
Rock climbing, abseiling and hiking. Travel.
**How?**
MBA in business studies. Previous corporate experience.
**Why?**
Because I want to make a difference and believe I can.
**Who?**
Don't know.
**Who else?**
Don't know.

> **EXERCISE**
> Use the questions from the two examples above to draw up and complete a *Logical Levels* diagram for yourself. We will revisit this diagram later, so keep it somewhere safe.

Remember that the best way to think of this is as a model that helps explain why people behave the way they do. This model though is not the real you. It is simply a representation on paper of who you have chosen to be so *far* this lifetime. If you had made different choices you would have a different model. It is useful in terms of establishing where you are starting out from.

When I attended the NLP workshop I guess I wanted something different from my life. I had a good lifestyle, satisfying work, was financially secure and had a harmonious and caring relationship, but at some level I wanted more. When I thought about it, I found that I wanted to be more than I currently was; I wanted to make more of a difference.

All the people attending the workshop had different reasons for being there, but when I spoke with them individually I came to the conclusion that, at some level, all of them wanted something different from the lives they were currently living. It was just that some could better express what they wanted than others, and some had taken more time out for self-enquiry and so were clearer about what it was they wanted.

You too may be reading this because you want something different from your life. You may even know *what specifically* you want to be different, or you may just have a vague sense that you want something more or different. Either way it implies that at a deep level we actually believe that we are capable of something more.

We are. You are. I ask just one thing of you at this stage, and that is not to set any limits on who that 'true you' may be or what that true you may be capable of experiencing or achieving. As my guides told me several years ago: there are no limitations. Whatever we believe is possible is possible! Such is the wonder of this dimension.

## CHAPTER 2

# THE MAP

Jane, an attractive, dark-haired 27-year-old, was one of many clients who wanted something different but didn't know where to start. Jane was particularly concerned about her career and where it was heading — or, more accurately, where it wasn't heading. She had an appointment with me because she wanted clairvoyant guidance about her future. By looking at a person clairvoyantly (with my inner vision) I am able to see key factors in their life that are currently affecting them, their present life situation and the future that they are creating for themselves.

I should perhaps at this stage point out the difference in the way that I am using the terms 'life' and 'life situation'. Our life is what lies within us, capable of infinite forms of expression. Our life situation is the situation we find ourselves in *at a point in time*. We all have infinite potential, no matter how bleak our current life situation may be. A good clairvoyant can help you see why things are happening in your life situation, and help you access more of your life, that divine energy that lies within you, to transform your life situation in the way that would suit your highest good.

I have worked clairvoyantly now for over 11 years and have learned that it is very rare for a future event to be set in stone.

Years ago, long before I had any inkling of abilities myself, a clairvoyant told my aunt that her granddaughter would never marry. This worried my aunt considerably at the time, but even more so when the granddaughter became engaged to be married. The couple were very much in love and my aunt was worried that one of them was going to die or be involved in a terrible accident. The day of the wedding came and my aunt sat in the church waiting for the groom to arrive, and then for the bride. When both had arrived safely my aunt couldn't help wondering if one of them was going to drop dead in the church during the service, or if someone was going to speak up opposing their marriage.

Of course, neither bride nor groom collapsed. The wedding ceremony proceeded beautifully and they were married. The clairvoyant my aunt had seen had got it terribly wrong and caused untold anxiety and distress to the family.

Over the years I have heard many similar stories, where clairvoyant ability has either been abused or misunderstood. What my aunt must have been through was at the forefront of my mind when I started exploring my clairvoyant abilities, and the responsibility for using these correctly is one I take very seriously.

When I first started exploring my ability I was curious about clairvoyance. In particular, I wanted to understand what clairvoyance can tell us and what it can't. In other words, what is destiny, and what is determined by our own free-will choice?

The future is created by the choices we make in the present. The better clairvoyants understand this and help their clients to understand it too. Once you know that you are creating your own future by the choices you are making right now, a clairvoyant can usefully help you to identify other possible choices, and thus other possible futures.

As I looked at Jane's life situations, past, present and future, I saw quite a bright career path that had stayed at the same level for some time. I saw Jane looking around for where to tread next. Her feet had seemingly come to the end of some kind of path. The light within her was brighter than the path she was on, and brighter than the people who stood around her a few metres away from the path. I took these people to be Jane's work colleagues and noted that I could not see any meaningful connections between Jane and those she worked with. I also saw a flash of glossy newspaper-type print.

The information had been clear and quick, so I relayed what I had seen to Jane. Jane confirmed that her main reason for coming to see me was because of her career. She had worked for the same magazine for several years and felt that her career had reached a plateau. My description of a bright path that had stayed on the same level made sense to her. As she saw it, there was seemingly no opportunity of a promotion where she currently worked and, because her husband was so well established in the local area, moving somewhere else just wasn't viable. She enjoyed her job but she wanted something more.

'I just feel so stuck,' she sighed.

'You are,' I agreed. I caught a look in her eye that said

'I didn't pay you to tell me that.' I smiled. She didn't.

'I can see that you have been looking around you to find a way onwards and upwards, looking for job adverts and keeping your ear to the ground.' She agreed she had. 'But you haven't found a solution, and you won't unless you do something different.'

'What do you mean?' she asked. 'I have tried everything.' I could see clairvoyantly that she had.

'What you need is a new map,' I said as reassuringly as I could while trying to maintain a straight face.

'A what?' she asked. I could contain myself no longer. I had to explain. It took me a little while.

I use the analogy of a street map with many of my clients to help them see their life more objectively and from a broader perspective. 'Imagine you have a street map of the town or city where you live. The map is not the town or city; it is simply a representation on paper of the streets and layout of the place. Internally, you will also hold a representation of the place where you live, an internal map of what the town or city is like. Your internal representation may be richer than the one on paper because it may include how buildings look and how places feel, but it is still a representation, not the real thing.'

Jane nodded that she understood, so I continued.

'Places you know well, such as your home, would be in good detail. Other parts you may find are in less detail because you have perhaps not seen them or spent as much time there. My map of your town or city would undoubtedly be less detailed than yours because you live there and I don't. I may not even know your town or city exists, and you may not know that the area I live in exists.'

I was reminded internally of a teaching I had received previously: *Just because I do not know a thing exists does not make it cease to exist*. A reasonable enough statement if you think about it, but how many people base their lives and decisions on the opposite view?

My explanation to Jane continued. 'A street map is usually used to help us find our way from one place to another. Its value is determined by how accurately it represents the territory. If it isn't accurate or complete we may well end up getting lost, and find ourselves somewhere where we really didn't intend to be.'

'I think I understand what you are saying, but what does all this have to do with me finding a new job?' Jane asked.

'In the same way that we hold an internal map of what the town or city where we live is like, we also hold an internal map of what life is about. All of our maps are different because we have all had different life experiences and hold different views. No one map is 'right', but more maps tend to be better than fewer maps because we can learn from each other's maps. Just like the street map, our internal map about life needs to correctly represent the territory, otherwise we run the risk of getting lost and ending up in a place we don't want to be. This time though the stakes are much higher. We are talking about your life!'

'So what you're saying is that my map may not include jobs that are actually there, just because I do not know about them?'

Jane was beginning to get what I meant. But there was more to it, so I continued. 'Partly, but more importantly there may also be more suitable jobs for you than you are currently in, ones you would find more satisfying.'

'Like what?' she asked.

'That all depends on the rest of your map and what you really want out of life.'

We spent some time exploring and challenging Jane's map of reality and what she really wanted out of life. Sometimes I used clairvoyance and sometimes I simply asked Jane questions. By the end of the session she was much clearer about what she wanted out of life and where she wanted to go with her career. The answers had been there all along — she just needed help seeing them. She needed a new map.

We all have different maps of what life is about. What determines a map's usefulness is whether it gets us to where we want to be.

On a more spiritual level, to open the door that Tony, the late husband in Chapter 1, referred to, we have to know that the door exists. It has to be on our map, so to speak. We also need to know that it is capable of being opened, and that it is capable of being opened by *you*. Otherwise this would all be a waste of time.

Through my television shows and live demonstrations of mediumship I aim to demonstrate that the doorway through to the other dimensions exists, and that it can be opened. But can it be opened by you? I know it can, but you may not know it can yet. All that separates my knowing from yours is time. Sooner or later you will realise (real-ise — make real, and real-ise — real-eyes — see with real eyes) what I already know — that you too can open the door. It isn't that difficult to do.

Our maps often change in response to our life experiences. Sometimes we can have experiences which cause us to re-write whole sections of our maps, as I found out about a year ago.

I had decided to take an art class so that, in time, I will be able to draw the faces of the loved ones I see in spirit form and provide additional proof of their survival. I was surprised that such a simple decision would create a whole series of events that would cause me to extend and re-write my map of reality in more than one way.

Despite living in New Plymouth for the best part of five years, I had never visited the local polytechnic before. It was strange driving to a new part of town, and I realised that I had not been inside a polytechnic-style building for over 20 years — in fact, not since I studied banking. They hadn't changed much from how I remembered them. They still had the same 1960s design and the same distinctive, musty smell, a mix of disinfectant and . . . My visit brought back a flood of memories.

Our class was quite small, mostly women, which helped us get to know each other quickly on the first evening. The teacher, a truly inspiring woman and wonderful artist called Donna Willard-Moore, held the belief that everyone could draw. I didn't share it. It was Donna who, at a social gathering, had first suggested that an art class might help me if I was serious about drawing spirit faces. I agreed to attend a short evening course, just to see if I had any potential at all.

At the start of the first evening class we took turns talking about what we wanted from the classes, and our experiences of art so far. We each had a story to tell and I found these both humorous and sad. I recounted that, as a child, I used to love drawing and painting, but that a good chunk of my enthusiasm for art had disappeared somewhere in adolescence, when my work never looked sufficiently like the 'real thing' no matter how hard I tried. I found that I could vividly remember a schoolmate who could draw well.

Michael Hurman was left-handed and had the most beautiful handwriting; art was where he truly excelled. While the rest of the class was struggling to get both sides of the glass bottle looking anywhere near symmetrical, Michael's bottle was three-dimensional; you could see the reflections in the glass and even see through it to the appropriately distorted faces of the students sitting across the table from him. It was as though you could have picked the bottle up off the paper. It was amazing. I gave up hope of ever being as good at art as Michael Hurman, and I suspect several of my classmates gave up at that time too.

As each of us told our stories, it became increasingly clear that none of us felt we were artistic. All of us had written ourselves off as 'artists' in childhood perhaps because of one experience such as my own that we still carried with us. As an 11-year-old I had decided that, because I couldn't draw like Michael Hurman, I was therefore no good at art. Now, with Donna's help, I was re-evaluating that experience.

'Many children get discouraged with art around the age of 11 when their art fails to look sufficiently like the real thing,' Donna explained in response to hearing my particular story. 'That's the stage when a good art teacher teaches perspective.'

I could have hugged her. Suddenly I saw my school experience with new eyes. Instead of despairing at not being able to do what Michael Hurman could do, I was inspired for the first time to find out *how* he did it. If he could develop the ability, so could I. Drawing perspective was something you could learn! It wasn't a case of 'either you can draw or you can't'; it was a case of 'everyone can learn to draw and paint and we can all learn from the masters, the people who are naturally good at a particular thing'. We just have to break down what they do to understand *why* that works.

I felt silly because, in other areas of my life, for example when I was working as a trainer, I had done precisely that. I had made a point of finding the best trainers I could and working alongside them to learn from what they did. I could see that in adulthood I had learned from others, but I wondered just how many other things I had written myself off about as a child — sport, singing, writing, acting, playing musical instruments. So many things, just because as a child I considered I was not as good as someone else and therefore 'not good enough'.

Over six evening classes I 'learned' to draw and to paint to a level I was happy with, something I had never managed to do at school. I never imagined I could draw and paint so well. It took me several hours to get a picture to a standard I was happy with, but I could do it. My first oil painting, other than the oil painting I did by numbers as a child, turned out amazingly well. But, more importantly, I shifted a belief that I had held for 30 years — that I could not draw or paint to the standard I wanted.

That oil painting now has pride of place in my bedroom, reminding me to be open to what is possible. Just because I have held a belief all my life does not make it true. It may be true or it may not — or it may be just waiting to be replaced by a belief that is altogether more wonderful!

So, if you are thinking that you cannot see or hear the spirit world, cannot connect with your intuition or your guides, or do not know why you are here, watch out — your beliefs are perhaps as vulnerable now as mine were in that art class!

## EXERCISE
### Reflection
Describe a time where you thought you couldn't do something, and then found you could.

Describe your feelings when you thought you couldn't do it, and your feelings when you found you could. What caused you to attempt to do it?

### Understanding
What can you conclude about your own experiences? What did you learn?

### Planning your next step
How can this knowledge or understanding assist you in the future?

As much as possible in the text and exercises that follow, I will not tell you what to think. Rather, I will get you to *explore* your own thoughts and experiences, your own maps if you like, so you reach your own conclusions.

Your maps of reality may well be more expansive and richer than mine and I truly hope they are, for then you can share your insights and help me along my path. We are all on this journey together.

This book contains a process; I know it works because I have been through it myself. There are other ways; this is just one. The conclusions and experiences triggered by this process will be uniquely yours and I invite you to share them with me and others on my website at *www.jeanettewilson.com* if you would like to. There is so much we can learn from each other if we dare to share.

So, if we are to get anywhere this lifetime, we need a map of reality that will serve us well, one that accurately reflects the territory. Our maps are constantly evolving and they need to do just that. At any time there will be sections of our map that are incomplete. We need to recognise where there are gaps in our understanding and knowledge and use our own life experiences to complete them.

This is just the starting point, where we become conscious of our *current* map, of how we currently see the world and how we view our place in the world.

First we start with what we *know* to be true. I was taught this by one of my 'guides' very early on in my journey as I was walking through a park. It was a beautiful summer's day, with a very clear blue sky. I was watching the different people in the park and not thinking about anything in particular when a voice started talking in my head. At the time I didn't realise it was a guide talking to me; I thought it was just me talking to myself. (As time has gone by I have learned to discern when the voices in my head are my own and when they aren't. You will find more about how to discern the different voices for yourself later in this book.)

'What could I, hand on heart, say I knew to be true?' the internal voice asked. I thought and thought. There was actually very little I knew to be true. Much of my knowledge had come from others — society, the media, books, television, school and other people. What did I know to be true from my own experience of life?

I knew that love felt preferable to fear and I knew that, through life, I had found out more about myself.

'What else?' the internal voice prompted. I knew that my physical body got wet when it rained and felt warm in sunshine, and I recognised that to understand wet and warm I also had to understand dry and cold. I knew what peaceful felt like because I had known stress, and I knew what healthy felt like because I had also felt unhealthy at times.

I continued to think about the question and I was amazed at how little I truly knew. The great majority of my thoughts and beliefs were based on someone else's perception, someone else's map. What worried me more was that I also realised my life choices were based on these thoughts and beliefs. But what if they weren't right? What if my life was going in completely the wrong direction because of the inaccuracy of my map? It was a seriously worrying thought.

To help me, my guides suggested that I think about the question in a more focused way. Firstly, to think about myself. What did I absolutely *know* about me and then what did I absolutely *know* about this space/place/reality that I lived in.

> **EXERCISE**
> **Reflection**
> Think about it now for yourself. What can you, hand on heart, say you absolutely *know* to be true about you? Jot down your answers.
>
> What can you, hand on heart, say you absolutely know to be true about this space/place/reality? Again, jot down your answers.

For me, the answers were quite brief. Bear in mind that there are no 'right' or 'wrong' answers to these questions. You are simply starting to explore your own map. My map of reality at 32 years of age is shown below.

*What did I know about me?*
I was 32 years old, a woman, a partner, a daughter, a sister. I was loving, kind, truthful, loyal, optimistic, ambitious. I was healthy. I was intelligent. I knew that feelings and emotions arose within me from time to time and that, rightly or wrongly, I had learned to suppress them.

I had learned through experience that I loved fruit and hated marzipan. I had also found out that I loved learning and was a quick learner, relatively speaking, and that I was a good communicator. I also knew that I had experienced a sequence of events that I didn't yet fully understand (my experiences at the NLP workshop).

I had come to learn that my feelings were usually triggered by thoughts; if they were worrying thoughts I felt nervous and if they were optimistic thoughts I tended to be happy. And sometimes, even thinking positive thoughts, I could not make myself feel good.

I recognised that I did not make myself breathe and I could not stop myself from breathing even if I wanted to. It was also clear that my physical body had changed through time, and I was aware that my physical body built and repaired itself from the food, water, oxygen and sunlight I took in. I thought that was amazing!

There was also the dawning realisation that I tended to believe what I read in newspapers or saw on television.

*What did I know about this space/place/reality?*
I knew that I was on a planet called Earth some distance from the sun, that other planets also orbited the sun and that all of this was contained within what was commonly termed a universe.

I knew that I didn't know what existed beyond this universe, how it had come into being or who (if there was a who) had created it. I knew that it was a three-dimensional reality; that is, objects have width, depth and height.

I knew also that there is a physical law of cause and effect (you push a cup along a table and it will move other lighter objects in its path), that we have gravity (if you let go of a cup it will fall through space), that time is relative (work seems to last forever when it is boring and a hot date flies by!), that physical bodies do not last forever and that there are seasons and living things grow and die.

I understood for the first time just how little I did know — how incomplete my map of this reality was despite living in this physical body for over 30 years. I have to say it did unsettle me for quite a while until I understood that it was okay not to know.

### EXERCISE
**Understanding**

For now, take some time to consider *your* own map of reality and to recognise the areas of your map that are incomplete. Allow yourself to be comfortable knowing that you do not know it all — yet.

**Planning your next step**

Choose one area of your map that is incomplete and identify something you could do to help complete it.

# PART 2

# DARE TO BELIEVE...

that you are more
than you yet perceive
yourself to be

# CHAPTER 3

# KNOW YOURSELF

### Gnothi seauton [ know thyself ]

— CHISELLED OVER THE PORTALS OF THE ANCIENT GREEK TEMPLE AT DELPHI

Like many people, over the years I have wondered who I am. I realise that I have a personality self, sometimes referred to as an ego, that has likes and dislikes or, in extreme situations, desires and hatreds. I also recognise that some aspects of my ego have changed over time. Some even change from hour to hour — for example, I may want company one minute and not the next.

Is that part of who I really am? Or is that just my Sagittarian nature? Or part of being a woman? Or is it something to do with my hormones?

Certainly some characteristics of our 'personalities' seem to be more ingrained than others. For example, when I was growing up I went to school with twins who, in many respects, were very similar but the main difference between them was their attitude. I remember puzzling about it as a child. Why was one twin happy and cheerful and the other more prone to moodiness? As an adult this had continued to puzzle me.

The twins I went to school with weren't identical although they were very similar to look at. Was it because they had slightly different genes? Were they treated differently even though they were in the same family? I wondered if they had changed over the years, or whether their basic outlook on life had remained unchanged. Was the saying that leopards don't change their spots true?

I know that I have repeatedly been called an 'optimist' and yes, when I compare my outlook on life to that of others, I would say I tend to have a more optimistic outlook than most people I have met. It is a way of looking at the world that has served me well; there has been no incentive to change it and so it has remained with me pretty much unchanged.

I have often come across people who are more pessimistic in their outlook. They, not unreasonably, call their pessimism being 'realistic' and often describe my optimism as 'dreaming'. Their pessimism, it would seem, serves them well from their perspective. They don't get any unpleasant shocks because they see them all coming. They, like me, have no incentive to change. And so in this place, Earth, where we get to exercise our free will, we have optimists and pessimists of all degrees, and 'personalities' of all kinds.

What makes us who we are? What determines how we see the world? Is it astrology, the placement of the planets when we are born? Is it our genes? Is it our parents? Is it our upbringing? Is it our life experiences? Is it a combination of some or all of these, or something else entirely?

The *Logical Levels* that I learned about on the NLP workshop, and that you completed in Chapter 1, are a useful starting point because they can help us to see our behaviour in a new and perhaps more objective way. Our behaviour, how we interact with the world around us, is but one aspect of who we are. By examining *why* we behave in a certain way we can start to understand the 'me' we are presenting to the world. Perhaps by understanding ourselves better we can start interacting with this incredible experience we call 'life' in a more conscious and more empowered way.

Claire was a woman struggling to understanding herself, or at least struggling to understand why she behaved as she did. She was an intelligent person and all her logic and reason told her that smoking was harmful to her physical body, yet she couldn't stop. She was in the grip of her behaviour — or so she thought.

Claire came for healing for a completely unrelated matter, but she happened to confide that she would also like to stop smoking, and asked if I could help. She had tried many different ways of stopping, including the more traditional methods of changing routines, keeping herself busy, knitting and nicotine patches, as well as less traditional ways such as breathing cigarette smoke into a glass of water and drinking the brown-coloured liquid that resulted. She really wanted to stop smoking, she assured me, but she just couldn't.

Claire asked if I thought hypnosis would help. I had known people that hypnosis definitely seemed to help, and had also heard of others for whom it hadn't. I asked Claire what she thought the underlying cause of her smoking was. Over the years I have found that it saves an incredible amount of time to ask this simple question. You find that a surprising number of people do know the cause of their situation, be it health, relationships or financial issues.

From her response, it was clear that Claire had already given her situation considerable thought. She had identified the times when she smoked — after meals and sometimes in the evenings — and often it was when she was with friends who also smoked. She also recognised that it was not as sociably acceptable to smoke now as it used to be. Some of the friends she had started smoking with still smoked, and some did not.

She admitted that, even if all her friends were to stop smoking, this would not be sufficient to stop her as she felt the habit had become too ingrained over the years. In other words, the need to be sociable that caused her to smoke in the first place was not a sufficiently strong motivation to help her to stop.

Claire explained that she had tried different strategies to get her over her 'high risk' times. She had achieved limited success with some, but none had worked for any length of time. Sooner or later the 'bad habit', as she called it, returned. She was really at a loss as to what to try next.

If you consider the *Logical Levels* model of why people behave the way they do, you will see that Claire had previously tackled this issue on a *What?* (behaviour) and *When?* (environment) level. To get a long-lasting change she needed to work on a higher, or deeper, level. Exploring the *Why?* level would help her understand her motivation to smoke or stop smoking. This understanding could then be used to effect a change in her behaviour.

I hadn't worked with anyone to stop smoking before. Usually people come to see me when they have either a lot of pain that conventional medicine can't relieve or when they are terminally ill and have tried everything else.

I began by thinking about people I knew who had been able to give up smoking, and reflected on what I knew of those people. Many had given up overnight, after the death of a loved one from lung cancer. The experience of seeing a loved one die from cancer caused by smoking caused a shift in the fourth ring of the *Logical Levels* model — the *beliefs and values* or why people do what they do. The realisation that smoking kills must have really hit home much more strongly than the health warning printed on the side of cigarettes. Perhaps they didn't want to die that way, or perhaps they didn't want to die prematurely or leave their family behind. Whatever it was, somehow a belief shifted as they realised that smoking really did kill. With that deep realisation they were suddenly and strongly motivated to stop. The shift on the inner level rippled through and affected all the other levels, creating new behaviours that lasted. They may have used nicotine patches, or changed their habits to help alleviate the discomfort of stopping smoking. But the drive to stop didn't come from the patches or the change of habits — it came from deep within.

All Claire needed was a shift on a higher/deeper level — the *Why?* level or above. I asked some basic questions about her family history and smoking and soon ascertained that she had already lost a close uncle to lung cancer. If that hadn't stopped her I did not know what would.

A question popped into my head, and I knew it was not my own thoughts because Claire had not told me that she had children. I let the question come out of my mouth. 'How would you feel if your daughter smoked?' I asked.

'My daughter's not going to smoke,' she replied indignantly.

'Why not?' I asked.

'Because I won't let her. It's bad for you. It's addictive, it's smelly — and it's horrible. I am forever telling her that she had better not smoke.'

'When I was growing up my mum used to use a phrase "Monkey see. Monkey do". Have you heard that expression?' I asked. She nodded that she had. 'What if all you are saying to your daughter about smoking has less impact on her than what she sees you doing?'

Claire's face dropped. Her expression said it all. It was as though a small electric shock had rippled through her body. A shift had occurred and it had happened on the higher levels first.

Claire told me later that as I asked this last question all she could see in her head was an incident from her own teenage years, when her mum had caught her smoking. It was as though she was re-living the moment of being hauled into the house and hearing her mum screaming what she would do to her if she ever caught her smoking again.

Claire realised that her own mother had smoked and had constantly warned her against smoking, sometimes threatening physical violence. But it had made absolutely no difference — Claire had still smoked.

She suddenly realised that her own daughter could end up smoking too — that her own sins, as she called them, would be visited on her daughter — and that was something she just couldn't bear the thought of. She loved her daughter and she hated her addictive 'bad habit' as she called it. She did not want to see her daughter struggle with the addiction that she had struggled with. She was determined to do whatever she could to stop her young daughter from ever going down the same path that she had.

I am pleased to say that Claire chose not to smoke again. How easy it was to stop surprised both of us. There were still nicotine cravings along the way, but she found them much easier to resist than ever before.

This kind of approach would clearly not work for everyone, but for Claire it did. Claire valued her young daughter's health much more highly than she did her own and, more than anything, could not bear the thought of her daughter being caught in the trap of an addiction to smoking. For her, suffering the addiction was worse than the health considerations. She had hated herself for being addicted to cigarettes but loved her daughter more than she hated her habit.

She did not want her daughter to hate herself, as she sometimes did. She stopped smoking for her daughter's sake as well as her own. Whenever she felt a craving for a cigarette she gained the strength to resist by focusing on how she would feel if her daughter ever became addicted to cigarettes because of her own behaviour. Next to that feeling, the desire for a cigarette was nothing.

# EXERCISE
## Experience

Imagine walking a timeline of your life from your birth to now. You can imagine it in your head or, if it helps (and it usually does), physically pace the line out across the floor. Clear a walkway that is free of obstacles or, if you prefer, find a suitable space outdoors.

Start from your birth and move forward slowly into the different stages of your childhood, adolescence and then adulthood. It helps to have your eyes closed so that you can really imagine yourself going through the different stages of your life. You may want to do this with a partner, who can guide you and note down your observations at each stage.

At each stage, let yourself recall what life experiences you had, what behaviours you displayed, what skills and capabilities you had and what you believed and valued. Really allow yourself to become thoroughly absorbed in the experiences, thoughts and feelings of each stage of your life. Feel it as though you are really there.

You many want to look at 5, 10, 15 years and so on, or you may want to look at each year in turn. Take time to note down the most significant things you noticed at each stage of your life. The *Logical Levels* diagram provides a useful format to collate your findings.

## Reflection

When you have walked the timeline and noted down all your findings, compare and contrast what you have found. What has remained constant for you? What has changed?

## Understanding

Clearly, the things that have changed are not the 'real' you. But

> do you really know which of the other aspects that have remained unchanged are the real you and which may yet change?
>
> **Planning your next step**
> What implications does this new knowledge or understanding have for you in the future?

Over the years I can see that in many ways I have changed a lot, and in others hardly at all. Some of the changes in 'me' have been gradual, and others have been much more dramatic, like the change that caused me to become a vegetarian.

I was brought up in a Yorkshire family. Meat and two vegetables was the staple diet for dinner, with Yorkshire puddings on Sundays. As a young adult I simply did not feel full if I did not have my meat and two vegetables. I loved all kinds of meat, especially gravy made with the juices of the meat and the meat stews that my grandmother used to make. There was no way I could ever envisage myself becoming a vegetarian. Sure, I loved animals, but I loved meat too.

I became vegetarian only after reading a book by Stephen Turoff called *Seven Steps to Eternity* which, incidentally, is probably the best book I have ever read to explain the heavenly dimensions. In this book Stephen describes the scene at an abattoir and the fear that the animals feel before they are slaughtered.

It wasn't something I had ever thought about before. I suddenly had the overwhelming realisation that when animals die they are filled with fear, and that, when you eat their flesh, on a spiritual/energetic level you also ingest their fear. This wasn't something I wanted to do. I didn't want to be responsible for animals feeling so much fear, and I also didn't want that level of fear within me.

Of course, I had always known that animals are killed for us to eat but I didn't really ever *think* about what that meant. The images in my head and feelings in my body after reading that passage were sufficient to stop me eating meat for good. I haven't eaten meat since that day and I haven't ever been tempted. Meat now holds absolutely no attraction for me.

So, a new piece of information triggered a profound and sudden shift within me and it happened on a beliefs (*Why?*) level. Sometimes it is a person or a life experience that causes a shift, as this next example shows.

I was sitting on the grass taking part in a small group exercise as part of the NLP workshop. We were taking turns to help each other explore and challenge our maps of reality, or how we saw the world. Had we worked one to one and found something that looked odd in someone else's map, we could perhaps have got into an argument, with both people seeing something in a different way. With a small group, any limiting beliefs in an individual's map would stand out to the rest of the group, and the peer pressure would hopefully lead to a healthy debate, or at least cause the person to examine the beliefs they were holding.

The process enabled us to help each other to see the world through different eyes, if only for a moment. It was taken as a given that no one view was necessarily better than any other, and that more views were better than fewer. In other words, more maps are better than fewer maps.

The exercise encouraged the development of a broader perspective and resulted in the development of more realistic maps for the individuals concerned.

I was pretty confident about my map, and that how *I* saw the world was how the world actually *was*. I could see other people's limiting beliefs without difficulty as they talked about how they saw the world, and I was pretty sure that I wasn't holding any myself — well, not any obvious ones anyway. When it came to my turn to talk through my map it was my comment that I never asked for help that attracted the group's attention. I saw the eyebrows raise and heard the sharp intake of breath. I knew that the group had spotted something I hadn't.

'You never ask for help?' queried a woman in the group.

'Never,' I replied confidently. I didn't, not with anything — work, family, finances, private life. I worked through everything myself.

'But you have just taken on a new job with new responsibilities. Surely you will need to ask for help with that?'

'No. I just find out what I need to know myself. It's very similar to work I have done before.' I was very self-assured. In my mind I considered that I had all the skills and abilities I needed to excel in my new role. I didn't need any help.

A male participant interceded. 'That must take up so much of your time, doing it the hard way. Haven't there been times when it would have been easier asking for help?'

Yes, I had to admit there had, but the group's protestations that not asking for help wasn't a useful behaviour just couldn't move me. You see, not asking for help had served me very well. I didn't trouble my parents, my teachers, my boss or my friends. It worked for me. I was seen as effective and successful and at work I had been promoted because of this.

The group soon realised that they would have to talk to me on a different level if they were going to get anywhere. Simply arguing with me about whether my behaviour was effective or not was not going to work. I mean, I was very successful — a bank manager at 29. The behaviour had clearly worked for me because it had got me where I wanted to be. Why should I give it up now? The group had to work on a higher level, and that meant finding out what beliefs and values underpinned my behaviours.

Another woman changed the direction of the discussion. 'What does not asking for help do for you?' she asked.

'It shows that I am independent, can problem solve, do not need to rely on anyone.'

'And how does that help the teamwork in your work environment?' came another question almost before I had finished speaking.

I could see what the questioners were getting at but, to be honest, I didn't care about how the team was working. Teamwork had not been important to me. What had got me promoted was my personal achievement. The organisation promoted individuals, not teams, so that was my primary concern; how I appeared to the people who had the power to promote me.

My beliefs just weren't budging even though more of the

group had joined in to express their amazement that I chose not to ask for help. I could sort of see their point, that not asking for help might adversely affect teamwork, but still there was no incentive for me to change my behaviour. I knew my work environment and the situations I had faced, and not asking for help had worked for me.

A man picked up the discussion where the others had left off. He interceded in a noticeably calmer and more thoughtful way than the rest of the group. 'So, if I understand you correctly, your not asking for help is useful because it shows the powers that be that you are successful and competent and independent and strong?'

'Yes,' I said. At last one of the group understood me.

'But what if asking for help could make you even more effective, even more successful? What if one of your new team members knew something about the challenges facing you, and that knowledge saved you a lot of time finding it out for yourself?'

Images flashed through my mind. I had already had a strong clash of opinions with my new boss. He was nothing like any other boss I had experienced, and I did not know how to handle him. And there had been other examples. What I was seeing overwhelmed me.

The man from my group had a point. I burst into tears. In a blinding flash I could see that I had made my whole life more difficult for myself than it need ever have been. I also saw in that moment that not asking for help from peers and bosses, and always doing things the hard way, could also be viewed as sheer stupidity by some people and so preclude me from further promotions. If the majority of this group of people could see something 'wrong' with my approach, surely others could too.

Suddenly I was freed of an awfully limiting belief that it was a sign of weakness to ask for help. And in that moment a second belief was also swept away — that it was not okay to cry in front of people. This had been drummed into me as a child, and here I was openly crying in front of people as a grown-up, and it was okay. Nothing bad had happened; instead, I released a lot of tension and felt the support of the group. I had allowed them to help me.

Later I understood that the beliefs were swept away simply by being brought into the light of my consciousness, my present-moment awareness. The moment I saw them for what they were they no longer limited me, and I was free of them. Until I could see the belief that I was holding for what it was, I could not let it go because I did not realise it was holding me back.

Sri Nisargadatta Maharaj said, 'You cannot transcend what you do not know. To go beyond yourself you must know yourself.' I was experiencing first-hand the truth in this statement.

Over the following days I felt myself softening, and allowed myself to become closer to members of the group than I had done before. All of this was invaluable to me when I started seeing the spirit world a few days later. Because then, when I most needed help, I was not afraid to ask.

Einstein once said, 'Problems cannot be solved at the same level of awareness that created them.' If you can rise above a situation, no matter what it is, and see it from a higher level of awareness, you can usually see what needs to happen to change it. With the *Logical Levels*, if there is a behaviour that you want to change you need to look to the higher levels, beliefs and above, if you want to create lasting change.

It seems to me that the 'personality' or ego that we present to the world is little more than an accumulation of thoughts and beliefs that we have acquired through this lifetime, and possibly before. Sometimes it seems that we change over time, almost imperceptibly. Certainly I can say this is true in terms of my confidence in speaking to groups.

Although always very self-assured on the inside, for many years I was very nervous about speaking in front of groups. Then 'life' presented me with a series of opportunities to face my fear of speaking in front of people.

The first opportunity came when I was a bank branch manager's assistant. My line manager had identified that I had management potential but didn't feel I was confident enough at expressing myself in front of groups or to the other managers. He was right, and recommended me for a position as a trainer at the bank's regional training centre. I was terrified — I might not be confident at speaking to groups but he didn't have to do that to me (!) — I reconciled myself to the idea by telling myself it was a promotion.

It was my first assistant manager position, and a big step forward in my career. Sandra, my new line manager, was wonderful and helped me through my initial terror by saying things like 'It is okay to be nervous . . . I was nervous too . . . Nervous means you want to do your best . . . It's a good sign . . . I would be worried if you weren't nervous.' She was a wonderful support and helped me by making sure the first courses I ran were to new inductees to the bank. 'They will know nothing about the bank,' she reassured me. 'To them you will be an expert.'

Experience taught me that she was right. Little by little my confidence grew, and soon I was training more experienced clerks. Within a year I was training people at my own grade, something I had never imagined I would be able to do. I grew to love training far more than banking, and although I returned to a branch for my second assistant manager post I seized the opportunity to return to training when the opportunity came to be a manager.

My beliefs about talking to people had shifted entirely because of my experiences. A fear of talking to people had transformed into a love of helping people to learn and grow. It was still quite terrifying to think that I would now be training bank managers rather than clerks, but I knew that my confidence would grow with time and experience, as it had done before.

Along the way I had to learn to accept my nervousness. This meant allowing myself to really *feel* the nervousness and let it be, rather than fearing it. I also had to have the experience of speaking to lots of different groups to really get the confidence that I could do that. Over time, my skill and capability increased, and very slowly this affected my beliefs about myself. These new beliefs, that I could talk to people from all walks of life, were rooted in reality, because experience had shown me that I really could do it.

By the time I needed to stand on stage as a medium, I was confident about talking to all manner of people, which is just as well as the mediumship takes all of my attention and focus. Becoming nervous in front of a group would be disastrous for me as a medium, as I have to be able to relax completely to 'receive' the messages.

When I look back I can see that my confidence in speaking to groups grew gradually over about 15 years, through lots and lots of practice. It wasn't something that just happened overnight. I learned that confidence doesn't just magically come because we want it. Wanting confidence just tells us very strongly that we aren't confident now, and makes us even more nervous. True confidence at a particular skill usually only comes through experience.

Sometimes a shared experience can cause the beliefs of a number of people to be affected all at once. The death of a loved one is possibly the most common example of this. I was living in England when Princess Diana died. I saw the shock of her sudden passing affecting a whole nation. People wept openly in the streets. I even saw grown men crying, something that I had never witnessed before, and until that point could never have envisaged. The British 'stiff upper lip' value was suddenly less important for a great many people than the need to express their feelings, and I saw new behaviours in England that I had not seen before. The change of beliefs caused a shift in behaviours.

When you look at the whole Diana and the Royal Family situation from a values perspective it is very interesting. Diana clearly held different values from the rest of the Royal Family and, simply by holding these different beliefs about what she thought was important, she challenged them to examine what it was that they valued.

The whole Diana and Charles situation was front-page news at every opportunity in the UK. The newspapers in particular seemed to take sides and to encourage the public to do the same. In truth, neither Charles nor Diana was 'right' or 'wrong'. They simply held different beliefs and values. By allowing that difference in values to be seen on the world stage they caused a great many people to examine what they believed and valued without having to go through what Charles and Diana and their families went through.

Diana's death, as shocking and painful as it was, caused a great many people to re-evaluate their lives and decide what was really important to them. In other words, it caused them to re-prioritise their values and make different choices in life, myself included.

### EXERCISE
**Reflection**

Think about a behaviour of yours that has changed over time — from a simple behaviour such as not eating a certain food to discovering that you like it, to life experiences that shook or reshaped your beliefs. Use the *Logical Levels* diagram to help you if you like. List as many changed behaviours as you can think of.

**Understanding**

In each case, consider the underlying belief or change in values that caused the behavioural shift. Was the change sudden or gradual?

> Were you conscious at the time of what caused the shift? Is there any difference in terms of how easy the various behavioural shifts were? Are there any patterns that you need to be aware of?
>
> **Planning your next step**
> What implications does this new knowledge or understanding have for you in the future?

It soon becomes clear that our beliefs and values change over time and, as they do, they affect our skills, our capabilities and our behaviours, the 'me' we present to the world. As we get older we may start valuing our health more than we did when we were young, and start looking after our bodies and eating better.

As you saw with the *Logical Levels* model in Chapter 1, the lower-order questions are *What do you do?* and *How do you do it?* Higher-order questions appear towards the centre of the diagram: *Who are you? Who/What else is there?*

The answers to the higher-order questions determine what we find in the outer circle. *Why?* is always more important than *What?* For example, if you prepare a meal because you have to, it will be very different from a meal prepared for a special occasion because you wanted to. Why we do a thing — our motivation — greatly affects the outcome of what we do. And the *Why?* is determined by our beliefs.

By bringing all of this into our consciousness we can better understand why we are like we are, and it is more possible for us to change. We cannot transcend or move beyond what we do not know. We have to *know* how we currently are and understand *why* that is before we can move beyond it.

From the preceding stories, and your own life experiences, you will probably realise that if we change a higher-order aspect we can reasonably expect to see the lower-order aspects to also be affected. But if we change a lower-order aspect, the higher orders usually remain unchanged.

It seems then that our beliefs fundamentally affect our skills and capabilities; if you do not believe you can do a thing you may never develop the skills to do it. Our skills and capabilities in turn affect our behaviour, what we are able to put into life and our interactions with this world. So, if that is how our 'personalities' work in terms of triggering behaviours, the next question we need to ask ourselves is — do the beliefs and values we hold serve us well? Or are there more useful and empowering beliefs that we could hold?

# CHAPTER 4

# NEW EYES

The voyage of discovery consists not in seeking
new landscapes, but in having new eyes.

— MARCEL PROUST

I was walking outdoors one day when a guide asked me to consider the following: 'What are the most beneficial beliefs that you could hold?'

> **EXERCISE**
> Think about this for yourself before reading on. You may also want to note down your initial thoughts.

I thought about it for a while and concluded that the most empowering beliefs I could possibly hold were:
*That I am a part of the 'All That Is'*
*That everything is interconnected and that I could affect the 'All That Is' through this connection*
*That all is learning*
*That there is nothing to fear*
*That this is a safe and friendly universe.*

The fact that the guide asked me what were the most beneficial beliefs I could hold implied that I could actually hold these new beliefs if I chose to. A thought occurred to me: if we choose our beliefs, either consciously or unconsciously, through life experience or new knowledge, perhaps we do not necessarily need the life experiences to create the new beliefs. Perhaps somehow we can just stand back from the beliefs we are holding and choose better ones.

This was a very exciting thought, one I was keen to experiment with. Did it mean that if I thought I could fly, I could fly? If I thought I could walk on water, would I be able to walk on water? A very firm 'no' came back in my head. My guide pointed out that my suggestions were not beliefs but thoughts and that, as they stood, they would not work. I could put them to the test if I liked. My guide clearly had a sense of humour, and there was clearly more to this concept than I yet realised!

### EXERCISE

Take a few moments to think about current beliefs you hold that you would like to change. Jot them down. Beside each one, perhaps in a different colour, jot down a more empowering belief that you would like to believe instead. For example, if *I cannot swim* is a currently held belief, *I can become a good swimmer* would be a more empowering belief.

You don't have to believe the new belief just yet — you just need to be able to identify what a more empowering belief would be. For example:

| Current beliefs | More empowering beliefs |
| --- | --- |
| I hate my body | I am happy with my body/I love my body |
| My finances are a mess | I am abundant in all areas of my life/ I am financially secure |
| I don't have any psychic abilities | I am psychic/I am developing my psychic abilities |
| I can't find my life purpose | I know why I am here and what I am here to do |

On the NLP workshop we used several different tools to explore and expand our beliefs. Sometimes we found that simply by re-wording a belief slightly we were able to cause a shift within us. For example, consider the statement *'I cannot swim'*. Say it to yourself silently and notice how it feels. Now try the sentence *'I cannot swim yet'*. Again, notice how it feels as you say the sentence to yourself. Can you feel the difference? I have heard it said that 'yet' is one of the most powerful words in the English language.

As I went through the workshop I noticed that some beliefs could simply be re-worded, but others couldn't. For example, if we take the belief *'I cannot swim'*, clearly we cannot just switch this to *'I am a good swimmer'*. Our whole being would reject such a shift. But we may be able to accept a modified wording of *'I cannot swim yet'*, or *'I am learning to swim'*. Either of these would be more empowering than the present belief, and would open up within the person the possibility that one day they will be able to swim.

> **EXERCISE**
> **Reflection**
> Take time to look at the current beliefs you have listed. Are there any that could be changed by adding the word 'yet'? Notice how simply adding one little word can transform how the belief feels.
>
> Look at the wording of your remaining beliefs. Can you modify any so that they are more empowering yet still true to the whole of your being?

Some kinds of beliefs can't be changed quite so easily. They need a different kind of approach, as this next story shows.

I had known Alex for several years. She had always wanted to write a book, but hadn't. When I returned from the NLP workshop I was keen to put my new skills to the test and Alex asked me if I would help her unblock herself from whatever it was that was stopping her from writing. 'I feel there is a book within me that needs to come out, but I just can't get it out,' Alex explained. She had talked with me many times before about her desire to write, and it would be interesting to see whether the tools I had learned at the workshop would help Alex to make the shift she felt she needed.

I began by fully exploring with her what the perceived problem was. 'When you say there is a book within you wanting to come out, do you know what it is about?'

Alex nodded. 'It's about families, and the importance of families.'

I could see there was more she could tell me, and that the subject of the book was clear to her. 'And when you say you can't get it out, what do you mean?'

Alex's response almost erupted from her: 'I am thinking about the characters in the book and the story line and the messages in the book almost all the time. I just don't get around to putting pen to paper.'

'Why not?' I asked, curious that she hadn't made a start.

'Life just seems to fly by, what with the children and groceries and housework and helping my husband with his business. There just aren't the hours in the day.'

I knew what she meant; she did already have a full life. Was that what was stopping her then — time? There was only one way to find out and that was to ask. 'So how much time would you need to write a book?'

There was a silence while Alex reflected on my question. 'I think I would like to write in blocks of time. I don't want to be breaking off and having to start all over again. A three-hour block of time would be ideal.' Alex nodded. Yes, she had made up her mind she would need a three-hour block of time.

We spent some time talking about her existing schedule and found that, by rearranging some of her work, Alex could leave herself three hours on a Wednesday afternoon to write. It was starting to look more like a time-management issue rather than a belief that was holding her back.

Just to check, I asked one more question. 'Okay, so we have agreed that by moving some of your other work you can create a three-hour window to start writing, and that you can do that from this week. Is there anything else then that would be stopping you from writing your book?'

Alex thought about it for a moment and I could see colour coming to her cheeks. 'I wouldn't know where to start,' Alex blurted out and it felt as though a whole raft of energy had been released.

'What do you mean?' I asked.

'It's such a huge undertaking writing a book. I wouldn't know where to start,' Alex despaired.

'But if you did know where to start?' I asked, excited that we may now have found the real belief that was holding her back, evidenced by the energy rush that had brought colour to her cheeks.

'Oh then I would be writing all the time, not just in the three-hour period we have identified but when the kids have gone to bed — in fact, any time I got the chance.' Alex's whole demeanour had changed; now she was enthused with the prospect of writing her book.

And this is how it often is for us. We think time is the problem for our not doing something, like going to the gym, going to the beach or spending time with our loved ones. But underneath, there is another reason entirely. The lack of time is just a smoke-screen; an excuse. By using the questions 'What is stopping you?' and 'If you did have X how would that be?' we can cut through the excuses to the real reasons that underlie the behaviour.

Alex's situation still needed some assistance, so I helped her to challenge her belief that she didn't know where to start. 'If you did know where to start,' I gently enquired, 'where would that be?'

Alex's response was almost immediate. 'I guess I would

start by writing a short version of the whole story and then divide that into chapters.'

'That sounds good to me.' I smiled enthusiastically. 'Then what would you do?' I asked.

'Well, I would flesh out each of the chapters, adding descriptive passages to really help people feel what it was I was trying to convey.'

'Are you sure you don't know where to start?' I had to ask. Alex smiled. She hadn't realised until then that she had known where to start all along. It was only her belief that she didn't know where to start that was holding her back. Simply asking questions that broke the task down into smaller chunks helped her to see the project in an altogether less formidable way.

There was just one thing I needed to check — that we weren't dealing with another excuse.

'So you have the time to start writing your book, and you have an idea of where to start. Is there anything else stopping you from writing your book?'

'No,' Alex giggled. 'There's not — only you taking up my time,' she said jokingly.

'There's just one more thing then,' I said, getting ready to leave. 'For most people the first stage of writing a book is thinking about the plot and developing the characters, and you have been doing that for years. So you really started writing your book a long time ago. This is just the next stage in the process.'

Alex beamed. She hadn't thought of it like that before. Her book was already under way — now all she had to do was write it down.

When we truly look at the things that seem to be holding us back, many of us see that they aren't really holding us back at all — we just *think* they are. Once we explore our blocks *consciously* we see them for what they are. We see them, if you like, with new eyes.

> **EXERCISE**
> **Understanding**
> Revisit the current beliefs that you listed in the previous chapter. Use the questions 'What is stopping me from. . .?', 'What would I want instead?' and 'If I had that, what would be stopping me from. . .?' to help you to understand your beliefs better and to identify any excuses masquerading as reasons.
>
> **Planning your next step**
> Now you know how to separate an excuse from a reason, how can you use this new knowledge in the future?

Sometimes a firmly held belief can be dislodged by finding evidence to the contrary. Matt was the boyfriend of a young woman I had taken up on stage with me. He had joined his girlfriend on stage to support her while she received a message from her late father. Matt was in his mid-20s and had a friendly disposition. I was part way through giving his girlfriend her message when Matt's spirit relatives decided to intercede.

Now, in my head when this happens it is quite comical. You could easily be forgiven for thinking that they have no manners. But it isn't that at all, it is just that they are so keen to help their own loved ones. I have learned not to be too hard on them, but

I still have to have a way of working that honours each spirit in turn, or no one would be getting any messages.

I had to ask Matt's grandfather, and whoever else was with him, to stand back for a while so I could finish passing on the girlfriend's message first. It didn't take long, and then it was over to Matt's grandfather.

From the spiritual side, the grandfather could see that the relationship was strained. I couldn't pass that on in front of an audience, so I kept listening. Matt's grandfather showed me that Matt couldn't find his way. He had drifted from job to job and was seemingly unmotivated, and this was unsettling his relationship with his girlfriend.

I found some words to start the message off. 'Your grandfather on Mum's side is keen to talk to you.' Matt nodded, confirming that he had been quite close to his maternal grandfather and that he had died.

'He is showing me that you are drifting from job to job.' Matt laughed a little self-consciously and his girlfriend gave him a sideways look, nodding agreement. As I was talking, the grandfather was explaining that Matt wasn't actually unmotivated, because he spent hours making things in the garage. He just hadn't found the right kind of work for himself.

'You think you're lazy,' came out of my mouth. The girlfriend laughed and Matt agreed. I was shell-shocked — why did I say that? 'You're not,' the message continued. 'Look at how many hours you spend in that garage. You just haven't chosen the right work yet.'

All at once I could see what this was about. Matt's girlfriend had been telling him that he was lazy for so long that Matt was starting to believe it, and now it was affecting his behaviour and their relationship. Matt's grandfather had come through to present some contrary evidence. Matt's problem was not one of motivation — it was in his choice of work. Matt's face lit up, and he smiled at his girlfriend. His grandfather was right. He had never been lazy — he was just in the wrong job and he needed to change it.

> ## EXERCISE
> ### Reflection
> Examine your list of currently held beliefs. Are there any that there is contrary evidence for?
>
> ### Understanding
> We can usually find contrary evidence for many of the beliefs we hold about ourselves if we try. Can you see why you originally developed that belief? Can you see why the belief you are holding may or may not be true?
>
> ### Planning your next step
> How could you use this new knowledge to affect your future?

So now we have looked at just a handful of the many tools available to help us explore and expand our beliefs. How did you get on? Were you able to shift all the beliefs easily or were some easier to shift than others? Were there any that you could not shift? This next section may help you to understand why that is.

As I went through the NLP workshop I noticed that not

everyone could take on the same beliefs with ease and that, sometimes, taking out one belief caused a whole series of other beliefs to be changed. This triggered a real shift in the 'personality' the individual was presenting to the world. When this happened it was quite magical to observe and, as far as I could tell, the changes lasted. From working with a great many people after the workshop, including myself, I learned that new, more empowering, beliefs can only be accepted if all other higher-order beliefs are in alignment.

For me, that helped explain why positive affirmations such as 'I am loved', ' I am healthy and whole' or 'I am safe' sometimes work and sometimes don't, and why I still cannot fly or walk on water!

If the new belief happens to be in alignment with all our other beliefs — great, there is an immediate shift. But if not, saying the statement over and over to ourselves seems to make little difference.

Andrew, my partner, came across this on a workshop he attended some years ago. The workshop had run over three days. The first day he arrived home feeling fine, but the second day he arrived home feeling awful. There had been a real shift within him and it hadn't been for the better. He looked grey.

After dinner, we set about finding out what had gone wrong. Was he ill? Had he picked something up from another participant? What we found took us both by surprise.

Andrew had only started feeling bad towards the end of the workshop. There were no physical symptoms; he just felt awfully low in energy, not like he usually did, and very, very sad. I asked about the last exercise of the day, and Andrew explained that it was simply about loving yourself. The tutor had demonstrated a technique and then the group had divided into pairs to try the technique out for themselves. They had worked with the affirmation *'I love myself'*. They had asked that it be accepted within them, and tested its acceptance with a body wisdom test.

Body wisdom tests are used by a range of therapists to check for food allergies and intolerances and can also be used to check what beliefs a person is holding. There are two methods of doing these tests. The first is where the client holds out an arm (not the one they write with) at shoulder height and to the side. The therapist then presses down on the arm, using reasonable force, and the client resists. If the client is holding a food that is good for them in their other hand, the outstretched arm is strong and can resist the pressure exerted by the therapist. If the food is one that would be harmful to the person the arm weakens and can easily be pushed down.

The second way is one you can do by yourself. You put your thumb and index finger together — and try to maintain a connection between them while placing the thumb and index finger of your other hand within the loop they make and pushing outwards. If you manage to keep the loop intact the food you are thinking about is safe for you, and if the loop breaks the food is harmful to you. Both tests can also be used to test a belief.

> ### EXERCISE: Body wisdom test
> Try it for yourself if you like. Start with a couple of statements that are true, such as your age or where you live, and then try one that is false. Notice what happens. Now try '*I love myself*' and see what happens.
>
> ### Reflection
> What happened?
> How do you feel about what happened?
>
> ### Understanding
> Most people are surprised at the accuracy of the body wisdom test. It is something we really have to experience for ourselves, and it can help us understand the extent to which our minds and bodies are inextricably intertwined.
>
> ### Planning your next step
> Think of *three ways* you could use the body wisdom test in the future.

When Andrew attended the workshop, much to his surprise he 'failed' the body wisdom test for '*I love myself*'. His finger and thumb just wouldn't stay together. Testing for beliefs in this way is actually very useful, but it was what happened next that caused the problem. Attempts were made to change Andrew's beliefs so that he could eventually get a positive test result for '*I love myself*'. It took some time but, after much perseverance, a positive response was obtained.

The exercise had seemed innocent enough on the face of it

— after all what is wrong with people loving themselves? But when I asked for guidance after dinner that evening a different picture emerged. Prior to the exercise Andrew had held the belief that he was love. In changing this to *'I love myself'* he had caused an internal separation, creating a separate self.

When you love yourself, this implies a separate *I*. It was not something that either of us had thought about before. As soon as the original belief *'I am love'* was reinstated, the awful feeling Andrew was experiencing disappeared, and his energy returned to normal. No real damage had been done, but the two of us had learned something very interesting about beliefs. You can't insert a new belief just because you want to. There has to be a more holistic approach.

It seems that we need to have all of these things: an awareness of our currently held beliefs; an idea of what more empowering beliefs would be; an understanding of how our beliefs are structured; and, ideally, some knowledge of what our higher or core beliefs are. Core beliefs are the beliefs that underpin all others. Sometimes we only discover that we hold a particular core belief by accident, as I did.

When I attended the NLP workshop one of my beliefs that I was conscious of was that I didn't *feel* things as strongly as some people did. There was a girl on the workshop who was very passionate about things and I wanted to be able to experience the depth of feeling that she seemed to have. She seemed more enthusiastic, more energised, more passionate than I was. I guess I thought that if I could feel what she felt I would feel more 'alive'.

When the opportunity came to experience a feeling more

fully in one of the exercises that the trainer was demonstrating, I chose joy. I wanted to feel more joy because, at that stage in my life, joy was a stranger to me. I had felt happy, but never filled with joy, and that was what I wanted to experience.

The trainer took me through an exercise that helped me to feel absolute, complete joy. It was incredible, and people told me that I seemed to float out of the room that evening. The feeling of joy went way beyond what I had ever conceived I was capable of feeling. *I* was the joy. It was not just something I was feeling; it was what I *was*. There was no separate me experiencing the joy.

But instead of changing my belief from *'I don't feel things as intensely as other people'* to *'I do feel things as strongly as other people',* as I might have expected, something else more profound happened, and my life changed immeasurably. The following day I saw my grandfather in the spirit world for the first time, and within 48 hours I was able to see literally hundreds of spirits.

It was years before I understood the true significance of this simple exercise that had taken just 10 minutes or so to complete. When I reflected on the experience, the only conclusion I could reach was that somehow the exercise had affected one of my core beliefs, one that underpinned many others, because many beliefs were swept away all at once. I didn't understand *how* it happened; I only experienced that it had. I found myself with many new beliefs — that it was safe to volunteer, safe to stand in front of a group, safe to feel my feelings, safe to be myself.

Once I had this realisation that a core belief had been

shifted, I started reflecting on what my core beliefs might be and what would be the most empowering core belief to hold. This time, though, it wasn't because a voice in my head had asked me to. It was because, through logic and reason and life experience, I had reached the conclusion that I must hold core beliefs that underpinned all others, and that if I knew what these core beliefs were I would be a lot closer to understanding who I was.

After much deliberation I came up with only two:

'This is a safe and friendly universe' and

'All is One'.

I have to say it didn't seem like a lot at the time. It was only several months later that I came across a quote by Einstein that said, *'The most important question we can ask ourselves is this . . . Is this a safe and friendly universe?'* I found myself grinning from ear to ear; perhaps I was on the right path after all. I was also reminded internally that my very first communication from the spirit world had told me that there was nothing to fear. I started to wonder if all our beliefs were rooted in either love or fear. And, if so, at the highest level, is that determined by our belief in connectedness or separation?

### EXERCISE
**Reflection**

Consider your current beliefs. Which are rooted in love and which are rooted in fear?

Which have at their core a belief in connectedness and which have at their core a belief in separation?

> **Understanding**
> If there is nothing to fear — no-thing, as in no substance to it — then that would mean that any fear-based beliefs are rooted in no-thing, an illusion. Is there a pattern to your beliefs in terms of which are rooted in fear and which are rooted in love?
>
> **Planning your next step**
> How can you use this new knowledge about beliefs in the future?

We have already seen that if we change a belief in the more central rings in the *Logical Levels* model it ripples out and affects all the outer rings. I started to wonder what would happen if I worked on the higher-level questions of *Who am I?* Or *Who else?*

Let's think about it for a moment. We will take two different scenarios, the first where we believe that we are a physical body separate from the rest of creation and the second where we believe that we are a part of something more powerful, an integral part of the whole of creation. How would that affect our beliefs and values, our skills and capabilities, our behaviours and our environment?

> **EXERCISE**
> Draw out two copies of the *Logical Levels* diagram and mark them Example 1 and Example 2. On both, at the very centre, assume there is a belief in something else, something grander which, for the purposes of this exercise, we will call the 'All That Is'. The ▶

> difference occurs at the next level *Who am I*?
>
> In Example 1 assume there is a belief that there is a *separation* from the 'All That Is', and in Example 2 assume there is a belief that there is a *connection* to the 'All That Is'.
>
> Complete the two diagrams thinking about how you would be if you held each *core* belief.
>
> ### Reflection
> How did you find that exercise?
>
> Was it easier for you to complete one example than the other?

When I did this exercise I found the following:

For Example 1: I am separate from 'All That Is', I value myself, my learning and my experiences. I value being the best. I value being financially secure. I value safety, survival and staying ahead of the competition.

For Example 2: I am connected to 'All That Is', I value my connectedness with all life, I value my feelings, my state of being, the whole of life. I value others, openness, trust and truth.

These beliefs and values then rippled out, affecting the other levels. So, for Example 1 skills and capabilities were orientated around looking after number one, being strong, and protecting the self. In Example 2 there was more co-operation, more concern for the whole, more compassion, more tolerance, more trust and more peace.

By the time I reached the behaviours level I found I was looking at two very different people. Example 1 behaviours revolved around getting what the individual wanted or needed, and Example 2 was more orientated towards working with others to achieve objectives that were good for the whole. In Example 1 there was no evidence of any environmental awareness and yet it was a significant part of Example 2.

So what conclusions can we draw? Your core belief of whether you are separate or connected determines much of how you perceive the world and your interaction with it. Notice how much more expansive the content of Example 2 is. If you believe you are separate from everything else it stands to reason that you would want to protect what you have, your feelings, your possessions, your life. You would value survival.

But if you know you are an integral part of the 'All That Is' you would value the whole, and your connectedness with the whole and your relationships. Those values would then affect your choice of which skills and capabilities you developed and how you went on to interact with the world.

It was in doing this exercise that I started to piece together *why* my experiences on the NLP workshop had affected me so very profoundly. I knew almost straight away that a core belief must have been shifted. Now, through doing this exercise, I was able to identify which core belief had been affected, and how.

The experience of joy was wonderful. So wonderful in fact that it caused me to let down my barriers to experiencing. I allowed myself to feel the feeling fully, and in doing so I experienced connectedness. There was no separate 'I' experiencing the joy; I was joy. On the higher levels those in the spirit world do not protect themselves in the same way that we do here, because there is no need to. Once my barrier to experiencing (my resistance) was down, it was easy for my grandfather in the spirit world to get through and make his presence felt. That was how I opened the door from this side for the first time. Then, when I had the experiences of seeing my grandfather and other spirit world beings, there was a profound shift in my map of reality, or how I saw the world. But I couldn't have that experience until I was open to it.

My experiences caused me to realise absolutely that I was more than this physical body, and that I had an eternal part that would live forever, as my grandfather and the other loved ones were evidence of. This new belief could be accepted easily because I was wide open at that time to the experience. Later on I also came to the realisation that my physical body was my vehicle for my time here on the earth and that I also had other finer energy bodies to experience other planes of existence. But more about that later.

At last I understood why the simple experience of joy triggered for me the profound change I have seen within me and in my life. The experience changed my map of reality from Example 1 to Example 2.

At this stage it is important not to take on my beliefs just because I say they are true. They are *my* beliefs, part of my current map of reality. My beliefs may or may not be true. So here is a version of the exercise I did, to help you have your own experience and reach your own conclusions.

## EXERCISE: Experiencing joy/love/peace/bliss

The aim of this exercise is to help you experience a positive emotion very intensely. You can choose from any of the above emotions, or choose one of your own. Just make sure it is a beneficial emotion, one that will make you feel good.

To create the feeling within you, you will be asked to recall times where you felt the chosen emotion strongly. You will also be asked to use your imagination to enhance the strength of the emotion within you.

### Experience

Start by finding a clear space a couple of metres square where you are comfortable to do the exercise. It can be indoors or outdoors. Select the positive emotion you wish to experience. Take a few deep breaths and close your eyes. Imagine that on the ground in front of you is a circle of pale blue flames. The circle is more than big enough for you to step into when you are ready. The pale blue flames are cool and come up only to your knees.

Standing outside the circle, think back to a time when you felt the desired emotion strongly. Replay the time in your head, remembering what you did, what you saw, what you heard and how you felt. Really let yourself *feel* the feeling.

When you can feel the feeling with the whole of your being, step forward into the circle. Maintain the feeling for as long as you can.

When the feeling starts to fade, step back out of the circle to the place you started from. Again, think back to a time when you felt this particular emotion strongly. It may be the same occasion or it may be a different one. Again, replay the occasion in your head. ❭

Remember what you did, what you saw, what you heard and what you felt. Really let yourself *feel* the feeling.

When you can feel the feeling with the whole of your being step forward into the circle once more. As you do so, the second feeling is added to the first, strengthening it. Maintain the feeling for as long as you can. When the feeling starts to fade, step back out of the circle to the place you started from.

Now you can either add more feelings from another strong memory or you can imagine how it would feel to experience that emotion even more strongly. Imagine how it would feel, what you would say, what you would do, how you would be. Really let yourself *feel* the feeling.

When you can feel the feeling with the whole of your being, step forward into the circle once more. Maintain the feeling for as long as you can.

When the feeling starts to fade, step back out of the circle to the place you started from. You can add as many memories and imagined feelings as you like until you obtain the intensity of feeling you would like.

When you think you have built up sufficient memories and imagined feelings to give you a really intense experience, it is time to test the circle out. First, you need to think about something totally unrelated to this exercise. Think about the funniest movie you have ever seen, or recall a favourite joke. This just breaks your chain of thought and feelings and allows you to see whether you can access the emotions stored in the circle when triggered.

When you are ready, step forward into the circle of blue flames and notice what happens. All the feelings that you have stored in the circle should come into your body. If the feeling is not as intense as you would like, take time to add more memories and imagined feelings and then test it out again. If you like, you can imagine a dial which when turned increases the intensity of the feeling by 10%, 20%, 30% or whatever you feel you need.

### Reflection
What did you experience while you were doing that exercise? How do you feel now?

### Understanding
Until I did this exercise I did not realise just how easy it can be to change our emotional states. This exercise really shifted something within me and, as always, whenever there has been a change within me it has usually been followed by a change in my life situation. This one certainly was.

Just experiencing a powerful emotion such as joy for a few moments can affect us in ways we may not even imagine. Think about the ways this experience has affected you. How may that affect the future you are creating for yourself?

### Planning your next step
How can you maximise the impact that this experience has on your life? How could you use this exercise, or the learning from it, to assist you in the future?

So far, if you have worked through the exercises in the previous chapters, you will have challenged yourself to believe that there is more to this reality than you have yet discovered, and that you are more than you yet perceive yourself to be.

Already you will have started to see that, by changing your beliefs about who you are, you start to create a new you or 'personality' self, and that this in turn starts to create a new experience of reality for you.

Once we understand that, by changing ourselves, we can change our experience of reality it is natural to want to play around with that concept for a while, just to see what is possible. That is precisely what I did for much of my young adulthood, using tools such as NLP.

I had already known life as a daughter, a bank manager, a mother and a medium. It seemed to me that I could keep on recreating myself and, in doing so, create a whole different experience of reality for myself, if I chose. But I had a very serious concern, one which increasingly niggled away at me as the years went by. What if all the 'self-work' I was doing was simply creating another false self, another ego that was just more like my current ego wanted me to be? I could keep on revisiting and rewriting my beliefs, creating that 'perfect' person with that 'perfect' life, but in doing so I would simply be creating another false ego to defend and promote. I wouldn't really be any further forward in understanding *who I was*.

What if there was *more* to who I really was and all the time spent doing self-work was actually taking me away from my true nature?

I like to think of 'life' as a playful interaction between ourselves and a loving universe that helps us understand, by bringing into the light of our consciousness, what it is that we are holding onto. By becoming conscious of the beliefs we are holding onto, we can better understand *why* something is happening in our lives, and not take it personally. We can then see whether the beliefs we are holding still serve us well. If they don't, we can let them go.

Through this playful interaction we can also start to understand the connectedness of all things. I feel this is the most important part. The fact that we can change our experience of reality by changing ourselves shows us just how inextricably intertwined we are with the rest of 'life'.

When we first recognise that this is so we often reach for the quick reward, creating a life for our self that suits our needs. But we could reach for something far more long lasting — an understanding of who we truly are.

Using the light of our consciousness, experienced in the 'now', we can use the opportunities 'life' presents us with to let go of any thoughts, beliefs and ideas about who we *think* we are. Then, and only then, can we start to experience our true nature.

# CHAPTER 5

# FINDING YOUR TRUTH

> Few are those who see with their own eyes
> and feel with their own hearts.
>
> — ALBERT EINSTEIN

When I was five years old I stood in front of the dressing-table mirror in my parents' bedroom and looked straight into my own eyes. I was on my own, and in my head there was a voice that talked to me. It talked to me a lot.

I asked the voice whether other people had such a voice in their head. The logical response came back that if they didn't they would think me very odd, and if they did they would probably think me very odd for only now recognising that I had a voice in my head. I was five after all!

I concluded, therefore, that the voice in my head must be the sound of myself thinking, and I didn't mention it to a soul. That belief may or may not have been correct. What I do know is that a lot of choices that I have made in my life were based on what that voice said. It was only many years later that I stopped to question whether the voice in my head was 'me' or not.

At 31, after discovering that I could see and talk to the spirit world, and realising that we do not die, I started exploring what other beliefs I held that may not be true. The belief that the voice in my head was the sound of myself thinking was one of the first to come under scrutiny.

What if that voice had not been me? What if it had been a spirit? After all, I had just found out that my grandfather's spirit had been with me for 25 years without my knowing. My grandfather had come into my energetic space when I was just six years old. He had just died and my father, his youngest son, had asked him to look after me. Instead of moving through into the spiritual dimensions, my grandfather stayed with me in my body. I had been completely unaware of his presence.

When I looked back on my life I could see that my grandfather had stopped me from doing many things I wanted to do. There had been times I had wanted to volunteer for things at school — to sing, to be in school plays — but hadn't. There had been times in class I had wanted to answer the teacher's questions but didn't. I could even remember a residential management course where I received adverse feedback for not speaking up in group discussions, because it had been clear to the trainer that I knew the answer. Internal battles had raged about whether or not I should do a particular thing. All along I had thought I was arguing with myself and had given the voices in my head equal weight. Now I knew

I had been arguing with my deceased grandfather, who hadn't wanted me to experience embarrassment or ridicule.

At first I felt a little cheated; all those missed opportunities. I had known nothing of his presence within me until he came forward that day in the NLP workshop. How could I ever know whether the voice that argued back with Granddad was me, or if that was another spirit? What if the conclusion I hurriedly reached at five years of age — that the voice in my head was me had been a flawed conclusion? Who or what had been running my life and making all my choices?

It was quite a disturbing thought, and I knew I had to somehow bypass the voice in my head to find the answer. Just knowing this brought the sudden realisation that, if I had to get past the voice in my head to know the answer, then clearly the voice in my head was not who I am.

We are not our minds. Our minds can be a useful thinking, planning and organising tool if used correctly, but all too often the mind is in control of us with its constant chatter and mental activity, stirring our emotions and taking us out of the present. Our mind takes up much of our energy and awareness with its constant dwelling on the past or worrying about the future, both of which are completely futile. We cannot change the past, and the only way of affecting the future is to make the most of the choices available to us in the present. The only place our awareness needs to be is *here and now*, in this moment, for that is when we are in our own power.

You have only to walk through any busy street or shopping mall to see how many people are 'in mind'. When you are in mind, you are not conscious. When you are in mind, you

FINDING YOUR TRUTH

are not in your power. Mind is actually taking you away from who you truly are, usually by keeping you very busy worrying about things that really don't matter. Why does the mind do this? Because, in doing so, it gets your energy and your attention. You feed it and it grows stronger. To weaken its hold you have to stop paying it attention, and instead pay attention to the moment and to experiencing the real you.

## EXERCISE

Set an alarm clock to go off at hourly intervals, and notice how often you are fully present as it goes off. If you are not fully present, simply notice that. Do not reprimand yourself for not being mindful; rather, be thankful that you have noticed that your awareness has wandered off into mind, and bring it gently but firmly back to the present. Notice the colours, the textures, the play of light, the temperature, the sounds, the smells, how you feel, what you see, the feeling of your body. Notice everything about the moment.

### Reflection

How often were you fully present? How do you feel about how often you were fully present?

A thought for you: If you are not your mind then just who has been running your life? Aren't you just the least bit curious? I was, so I decided to observe my mind for a while, and this is how I came across meditation.

Meditation is the best way to start to observe the mind and thus free yourself from it. As you will recall from earlier in the book, you cannot transcend what you do not know.

> The antics of my mind were quite amazing; it just didn't stop. The more I tried to control it the worse it got. Sometimes it would get really extreme, flooding me with irrational or angry thoughts, just to get my attention.
>
> The aim in meditation is to be present; to be fully aware of your thoughts, feelings, emotions, and external and internal sensations all at once. Instead, I found that my mind was judging all of these, creating a boundary between me and my experience of 'life' again, but in a more subtle way. How can I truly experience who I am and what 'life' is if I do not allow myself to fully experience either? How can I truly experience what is, if my mind insists on coming in and deciding what is good or bad, pleasant or unpleasant, constantly endeavouring to resist the negative?
>
> Slowly, using meditation, you come to see what the mind is doing, and you can stand back from it. The mind still does what it does but you are more aware of what it is doing, not judging it in any way. But you also become more aware of what *else* is. Your sense of self expands and so does your consciousness.
>
> **Planning your next step**
> Based on what you discovered in the previous exercise, what can you do to ensure you spend more time in the now?

Years ago I had a dream, one of my most profound dreams. I share it with you now in the hope that it will do for you what it has done for me.

I dreamt I was walking towards an image of myself in a mirror. I knew that as I let 'Jeanette' go I would see God/Light as a reflection. I made the journey towards the mirror, step by slow-yet-steady step, aware that my physical form was lying down behind me and that, in my physical hand, was a pen.

I knew God was there for me and that I was safe. The feeling was incredibly beautiful and profound (I use the word God to describe the grandest version one could possibly have of a consciousness that supports and loves all forms of Life and is omnipotent and omnipresent, a part of All That Is and All That Isn't). I felt my soul body leave my physical body; I was soul and I knew that I could go if I wanted to. I realised that the people left here, especially my family, wouldn't know what had happened to me and that perhaps they would think I had died. And I understood just how easy and beautiful it would be to die when the time came.

At a deep level I wanted to let the people here know about the process of letting yourself go, so that they would realise just how easy it was to find the God/Light within, so I returned to my physical body and the pen in my hand.

As I 'awoke' I felt twice as big as I physically am. I knew absolutely that I needed to be aware, moment to moment, of how much time and energy I was putting into keeping 'Jeanette' rather than God/my true self in existence. That is why we need to stay in the present, because only then can we become aware of what it is we need to release.

So how do we find this God/true or authentic self/light within?

William Shakespeare wrote: *'This above all: to thine own self be true.'* Implicit within this famous quotation is the belief that it is possible to know ourselves and thus determine how to be true to ourselves. To me, knowing my true self is not something that has happened overnight. It has taken years of self-enquiry and observation, and is a continuing process. I am aware of a deep resonance, a peace that comes from within me and fills me when my life is in alignment with all parts of my being. Conversely, and sometimes easier to identify, there is an underlying unrest or dissatisfaction when I know I am not being true to myself.

*Knowing* goes beyond the intellectual exercise of analysing using your mind. To me it seems we have to experience who we are on a level beyond mind because the mind, in itself, cannot give you the answers you seek. You are more than mind. This next meditation is designed to help you experience your true nature.

### EXERCISE: Meditation to connect with your true nature

This meditation starts with a guided visualisation to help you connect with the deeper aspects of *you*. You can either read this onto a tape to listen to, or ask a friend to read it to you. (For details of tapes I have already recorded, see my website, *www.jeanettewilson.com*)

Find a comfortable place to sit and ensure that you will not be disturbed by personal callers, phone calls or other interruptions. Sit comfortably, with your head and shoulders relaxed and your back straight. Feel the connection that your feet are making with the floor and the connection that the base of your spine and buttocks are making with the chair. (If you are sitting on the floor simply feel your connection with the floor.)

Notice your breathing; feel what it is like to breathe. Notice whether you are breathing from the top part of your lungs, moving your chest, or from the lower part of your lungs, moving your abdomen. It is best to breathe from the lower part of your lungs as this helps you to relax more deeply. Allow yourself to do this now, and breathe at a pace that is comfortable for you. Just breathe. Let your whole being slip into a rhythm of breathing that is comfortable for you. Take your time.

When you are ready, start noticing how your body is feeling. Starting at your feet, just let your awareness move into your toes and notice how they are feeling. You are not trying to change your toes in any way, you are just noticing how they are feeling. Holding your consciousness in your toes, allow them to relax. Allow your toes simply to 'be'. They do not need to hold onto energy right now; they can simply be and relax. Allow your toes to relax at a deep level.

Once you can sense that your toes have relaxed, let your awareness move gently into your feet, and notice how they are feeling. You are not trying to change your feet in any way, you are just noticing how they are feeling. Holding your consciousness in your feet, allow them to relax. Allow your feet simply to 'be'. They do not need to hold onto energy right now; they can simply be and relax. Allow your feet to relax at a deep level.

Once you can sense that your feet have completely relaxed, let your awareness move gently into your ankles, and notice how they are feeling. You are not trying to change your ankles in any way; you are just noticing how they are feeling. Holding your consciousness in your ankles, allow them to relax. Allow your ankles simply to 'be'. They do not need to hold onto energy right now; they can simply ❱

be and relax. Allow your ankles to relax at a deep level.

Once you can sense that your feet have completely relaxed, let your awareness move gently into your lower legs and notice how they are feeling. Allow your consciousness to move to each part of your body in turn, noticing how that part feels and then allowing it to relax. Once it has fully relaxed, move on to the next part, until the whole of your physical body is fully relaxed.

Allow yourself to sit with the whole of your physical body relaxed. Notice how it feels and how different this feeling is from your usual way of being. Inside of you, you will feel a feeling, a consciousness, a resonance, which is uniquely you. Let your awareness rest in the resonance, that deep feeling of who you really are.

Just allow yourself to be with that energetic essence of who you are. You are not looking for words or pictures. You are just connecting at a deep level with who you truly are — the energy or resonance at the core of your being; your true nature.

Experience your true nature for as long as you feel the need, and know that when you next do this meditation you will be able to connect even more deeply, even more clearly with the deepest part of your being. With each connection you will come to experience your true nature ever more deeply. Sometimes it will be on a conscious level, gaining new insights about who you are, and sometimes it will be completely unconscious. But always the connection between the you that you present to the world and the true you will be strengthened and enriched, for you cannot fail to be affected by the beautiful presence of your all-pervading true nature.

When you are ready, let your awareness start to return to the here and now, to the feeling of your feet on the floor and your connection with the earth. Know that the connection with your true self has

> been made and that the benefits of this connection are already filtering through to the you that you are presenting to the world, even if you are not conscious of that process.
>
> Allow your consciousness to return fully to your physical body, feeling all parts of your body. You may find it easier to move your fingers and your toes before opening your eyes. When your awareness is fully back in your physical body and you have opened your eyes, take time to reflect on the experience. Reflect on it as a *feeling* rather than trying to sum it up in words. Words will only limit the experience.

It is by connecting with this deeper sense of who we are that we find our way. For me, it is in the moments that we experience this deep awareness of who we are that we start to find ourselves. It isn't always restricted to the times when we meditate — 'life' gives us lots of moments when the real us comes through.

One of my most special moments was holding my baby daughter Sarah in my arms for the first time. I was in a drab and clinical hospital room, tired and sore after labour, but as soon as I held her it was as though the hospital room and all the pain of the labour no longer existed. For a moment, it was as though there were just the two of us, as though we were the only ones who existed. The core of my being was connected with the core of hers, and nothing else mattered.

At other times I have felt similar connections with my son Liam and my partner Andrew, and sometimes with people who appeared to be complete strangers. You may even experience this feeling with animals or with nature, especially in a beautiful space. Something happens and time stands still. There is a profound sense of connection and things are never the same again.

It is this deeply felt sense of who we are that can guide us through life — if we let it. Before I did my very first mediumship show, before I even set up the charity I was inspired to establish, I was well and truly stuck. I knew I had so much potential but I didn't know how to use it or where to focus my time and energy. So I started meditating. As a busy mum of two preschool children it was hard to find the time.

I found myself waking in the middle of the night and, rather than lying there waiting to fall back to sleep, I experimented with meditation. I would go downstairs, wrap myself in a blanket, sit very still and then relax my whole body, starting with my toes and working my way up to the top of my head. I found it was infinitely easier to meditate in the early hours of the morning when everyone was asleep than it was in the daytime. It was as though there wasn't the mental chatter of everyone thinking.

Information came through clearly and I was then motivated to do the same the next morning and the next. It got to a stage where I was very disappointed to wake up and find it was light outside and that I had missed my meditation time. During meditation I would sometimes experience a blissful state of being, and at other times I received a lot of information about what was happening on the earth, and teachings for me and for humanity generally. When I asked about why I felt so stuck I was told that I needed to align my life with my beliefs. It seemed so simple, and it was at first.

I had to compare what I believed about reality with how my life was. There were many glaring inconsistencies that raised some soul-searching questions for me.

If I believed that all life was valuable, why did we try to trap the mice that invaded our country home? If I loved the earth, why was I not making more of an effort to recycle? If I believed that I was an integral part of a loving universe, why was I not allowing myself to be loved? If I believed that everything always happened for the highest good, why did I not trust more? If I believed I was made of energy, why was I polluting that energy with the additives and preservatives found in processed foods?

If I believed family was very important, why wasn't I prioritising my time better so that I could spend more quality time with my family? If I loved my partner and wanted to spend the rest of my life with him, why was I less kind to him than to complete strangers? If I believed in my mediumship abilities and that I could make a difference, why was I not sharing with others what I could do? If I believed in higher aspects of consciousness that can help us, why wasn't I accessing them more?

The questions went on and on, and I realised that I was being very untrue to myself in many areas of my life. I didn't know where to start, so I started with the easiest ones. I started growing my own vegetables and recycling materials in and around the home. Then I moved on to being more kind to my partner.

In addressing each of these areas in turn, I somehow managed to unblock myself. Looking back now, I can see that I started to flow more of who I truly was, who I chose to be, into each area of my life and, by noticing the response, I was able to make new choices for myself and free more of myself.

My life started to change in profound and beautiful ways. My relationship with Andrew transformed almost immediately. I was kinder to him and he became more helpful to me, assisting me more in the home. My health improved; it had not been bad but I found myself with more energy and more mental clarity. Opportunities to practise mediumship and healing presented themselves with no effort on my part and, just as effortlessly, the idea for the charity began to take shape. The charity would be an expression of the things I thought I could usefully affect in one way or another.

It was several years later, when I was with a group exploring the phenomenon of channelling that I understood more fully what had been happening to me over that period. Channelling is similar to mediumship except that you connect with a higher aspect of consciousness, usually a more wise and loving being than you would ordinarily find on the spirit-world levels. They are unlikely to be a family member. Some do not have names and some appear to be collective consciousness, in that they appear to be more than one being. You will find more about channelling in Chapter 6, but for now I will just explain what happened in relation to the phase I was going through in my life.

One of the channelling group wanted to know if her desires and plans were in alignment with her 'divine path'. It was a question she had carried with her for some time. She knew what she wanted but, at some level, she wasn't sure if it was okay to want what she wanted, or whether that was simply her ego's desires.

The person who was doing the channelling for the group was seated in a relaxed position, with her back very straight and her posture upright.

The response came back almost immediately — 'You are your path'.

With this response came a complete and simple knowing: that who we are, and our paths, are inextricably and completely entwined. As you uncover more of the real you so your path unfolds before you. It made perfect sense to me, and it was as though a penny had dropped — now I realised why the trigger for my own experiences was aligning my life with my truth.

To unblock myself and find my way, all I had to do was align my life with what I believed to be true. The channelling had encouraged me to think about what I believed and to compare that with how I was actually living my life. It had challenged me to see whether I was living my truth.

The more I aligned my life with my truth, the more my life moved forward and the real me was given expression. The secret for me was small steps. I have found that my concept of who I am and why I am here expands as I unfold more of my own truth. Perhaps we need to keep asking ourselves these questions from time to time, to keep accessing more of who we truly are.

I also realised that what had at first seemed like unrelated small steps were all steps on the way to my bigger life purpose. It is worth mentioning that whoever it was I channelled did not tell me what to do, or what changes to make. They just got me to reflect on what I believed and how my life was. The choice of changes I made, the 'how' and the 'when', were all mine. That is usually the sign of a higher guide, because they know how we really learn, and so then we can apply the same principles again and again in different areas of our life.

> **EXERCISE**
> **Understanding**
> Consider your list of what you believe to be true, and compare it with how your life currently is.
> To what extent are you living your truth?
>
> **Planning your next step**
> Identify *three* areas that are the easiest to tackle. Decide what you will do, and by when. Plan the changes and then diarise for a month from today to reflect on what changed for you. Then plan to tackle the next three easiest issues.

Sometimes when we make internal, or even external, changes there is a time delay before we start seeing the results. This is because we exist in a physical dimension. It is like trying to change the direction of a wheel that is already spinning — it takes time.

In the higher spiritual dimensions you have only to think a thing and it is so. This dimension is more dense and our thoughts exist as thought forms before they come into physical reality. If we keep holding the same thought, sooner or later it will become a physical reality. But if we become distracted and start thinking about something else then it will take longer to manifest, and we may even end up manifesting something else instead.

It took me several years to release my financial blocks, and even when I had I didn't see the effect for a little while. I started to question whether there was more work for me to do. I couldn't find anything else to release but, sure enough, a few months later the evidence that I had released the blocks was plain to see. Money even started arriving in the mail for no good reason! But that's a book all to itself!

If you make changes and the results are not what you want, remember that life is simply giving you feedback. You are connected to the whole of life and if you make a change within you, you cannot help but affect your life situation. There is no need to take the feedback personally; the universe isn't judging you. It is impartial. *Learn* from the feedback. Reflect on it, draw conclusions about why you got the particular result you did, and then plan what you will do differently to get a different result.

If you like the responses you get, do more of the same. If you don't like the responses you get, change what you are doing. *Remember that insanity is doing the same thing over and over again and expecting a different result!*

One of the things that has helped me most along my path is the realisation that everything is connected. You see, if everything is interconnected then everything I do, think or say has an effect. If I am interconnected with this incredible experience we call 'life' I cannot fail to be on my path, because my path is redefined with every little step that I take or don't take.

My favourite quote of all time is by an unknown Indian author:

*'Life as it is meant to be lived is a sacred outpouring of action from the deepest recesses of the soul.'*

It is the driving force for the charity that I helped establish and now support: *www.thedharmictrust.co.nz*.

If our actions, our words and our feelings are motivated by the deepest part of our being, we will be living our lives in accordance with all that we truly are. We will be walking our sacred path and, in doing so, will become more of who we truly are.

To me, the real beauty of this way is that only *you* can tell if you are walking your path. Only *you* truly know whether the life you are living is in alignment with the depths of your soul. It therefore follows that only you know the way; only you hold the keys. You do not need anything outside of yourself to find your way, because the answers all lie within.

## Some channelling that fits finding your truth

When I asked for guidance myself some years ago from the highest level I had access to, this is what I 'received'. It resonated well with me at the time and still does today. As you read the passage, see how it feels for you.

> *Your personality self is a collection of fears and desires.*
> *Man is imprisoned by the cords of his own desires.*

*He is weakened by the pain and suffering
  his desires bring upon him.
There is no joy in the world of illusion.
True joy can only be found within.
Let the light within be your focus.
Let the path of love be your guide.
Love and light are here to help you.
There is no need to be afraid.
One by one we undo the cords of desire.
One by one your true needs will be met.
It is not the new job, new car or house that
  will make you happy.
And you know this deep within.
Listen to your inner voice. It does not lie.
It is your truest guide.
When pain and suffering abound in years
  to come\* you will need more than ever to
  be true to yourself.
Your true self, not the self you think you are,
Or others want you to be.*

---

\*Humanity does have some potentially difficult times ahead, but nothing is set in stone. We have free will to make the most of the situations that present themselves.

# PART 3

# Dare to believe...

that you have abilities you have not yet discovered

# CHAPTER 6

# RECEIVING GUIDANCE

Simon had been coming to a development group I was running for a couple of weeks. By day he was a baker, but throughout his life he had been absolutely fascinated by anything remotely spiritual or supernatural. He had an inquisitive mind and had explored everything from aliens, ascended masters, telepathy, palmistry, telekinesis (moving things using your mind), mediumship — you name it, Simon probably knew something about it or had had experiences with it. He was a welcome addition to our group as he had much information to share, and knew his own mind.

Throughout all his searching Simon still hadn't received any 'messages', as he called them, that he was even on the right path. He had been searching all his life and was 'peeved' in a sincere and kind way that I, who had displayed no interest in such things, could suddenly be able to do what I did, seemingly at will.

'Don't get me wrong,' he explained. 'I am really enjoying

coming to this group and am getting a lot out of it. But how come you get all these experiences when you weren't really that bothered about this kind of stuff, and I have travelled all over, done so many workshops looking for answers and guidance and I don't get anything?'

I shrugged my shoulders. I had been asked this many times before.

'I don't know.' For a moment we just looked at each other. 'I don't know why the things that have happened to me have happened. But I do know that whenever I have asked for a sign, each and every time that sign has been given.'

'What do you mean?' he asked.

I started to relay what happened when I really, really needed help. I had stood at the edge of Regent's Park lake, not daring to step on the water but knowing that I ought to be able to walk on it. It was a time that I had feared for my sanity, and I had begged for a guide to show themselves to me so I would know that what was happening really was for real and that I wasn't losing it completely. On the way home from the lake a guide came to meet me. He was a blind man, whom I saw from my train as it pulled into the station. I immediately suspected he was a guide and, to test him out, I deliberately went down a different underground tunnel to the one he had taken. Within seconds we 'bumped' into each other.

'That's just the kind of thing I mean,' Simon interjected. 'Nothing like that has ever happened to me.'

'That kind of thing has only happened to me twice,' I said, regretting the words as soon as they were out of my mouth. I was making matters worse. 'How about we do a meditation to find out why you haven't received the "signs" you are searching for?' I could feel the rest of the group's discomfort and my own too. I honestly don't know why I am helped as much as I am. I am just extremely grateful for all the help I receive.

I led the group in a guided visualisation to begin with, as we needed to clear the frustrated energies that had built up in the room and were making everyone feel uneasy. First, we each visualised a golden ball at the base of our spines and then a second, similar-sized ball at the centre of the earth. We then imagined golden light connecting the two balls, forming a tube of light that was a visual representation of our grounding cord. As energy beings we do have a connection with the earth and, by visualising it in this way, we help to activate it. We then checked that the tube connected securely at the base of our spine and at the centre of the earth.

Then it was time to send anything that no longer served us down the grounding cord. It might be negative energy, old energy, fear, doubt or, in Simon's case, frustration. In my case it was a sense of helplessness. I suspect more than one member of the group may have sent some embarrassment down the tube, because the situation did feel rather awkward. When we send any energies down the tube in this way the intent is that we let them go and that they are transmuted into more useful, loving energies that are then returned to us, coming into the top of our energy body.

Within a few moments the room was feeling much clearer, and the energies much lighter. I helped the group go through a guided exercise to connect with their 'Higher Self'. You will find the exercise they did in Chapter 9. When your Higher Self comes in, you feel noticeably bigger than you physically are. I noticed from Simon's posture and facial expression that he had a particularly strong connection with his Higher Self. All the frustration of a few moments before had vanished, and his face was peaceful and radiant.

'Allow yourself to sit with your Higher Self,' I continued. 'Feel the infinite love and wisdom radiating through you.' I could see that Simon still had a strong connection. 'As your Higher Self, look at what is currently happening in your life.' After a pause, 'What is it that your Higher Self most wants to tell you?'

As I looked around the room it was clear that each person was connecting with their Higher Self to some extent. Just how strong those connections were would be confirmed when we witnessed the qualities of the response they received.

After a few moments I guided the group back into present-moment awareness and gave them a few minutes to reflect on their experience. The information received may or may not be for the public domain. Sometimes it is appropriate for the individual to keep what has happened to themselves, while at other times people willingly share the insights they have been given, and this helps others too. I leave it to the group to decide what they volunteer, and when.

One by one they shared what they had seen and, in some cases, heard. When all eyes fell on Simon he said he hadn't experienced anything. I was crest-fallen. I had seen the physical changes in his body as Simon had connected with his Higher Self.

'Didn't you feel anything?' I asked incredulously.

'I felt bigger and lighter,' he explained, 'but I didn't *get* anything.'

Now I got it. 'You felt bigger and lighter but you didn't *get* anything?' I checked.

'No,' he answered with complete sincerity. In his eyes, he *hadn't* got anything.

'What is it you expect to get?' I asked, to help me try and see this situation the way Simon was seeing it.

'I don't know,' he said. 'A voice, an angel, a colour, just something that I know isn't me, something that shows me that there is something else, a higher wisdom.'

'What if that wisdom isn't in a form like us?' I gently enquired. This time it was Simon's time to shrug. I took that as a sign to continue. 'What if the higher guides are made of light?' I asked.

'I could feel plenty of light,' Simon said. 'But I didn't *get* anything from it, no words, no message, no pictures.'

'So you want words and pictures?' I asked.

'Yes,' he said.

'Next week then we will ask for words and pictures. We might not get them, but we can ask.'

The following week came around and I wondered if Simon would come or if he had already given up hope of ever receiving his 'messages'. But he did turn up.

We did the same meditation as before and again I observed as Simon and the others connected with their higher selves. This time, when it came to the part where we ask what our higher selves most want to tell us, I asked that the message be given in the form of words or pictures.

Well, that week there was no silent reflection. Simon could not wait to share what had happened. He had heard his first voice. It had been inside his head, a man's voice much gentler than his own, and it had said simply 'Your guidance is always with you — it is just not always in the form of a voice.'

The group were so thrilled for him, and bemused that the message saying that guidance was not always in the form of a voice had come through to him in a voice! Someone, somewhere, had a sense of humour!

The message encouraged Simon to keep on with his meditation practice, although it was a long time before he received another 'message' in the same way. In the meantime, he started to be more open to the many other ways his spirit-world helpers were helping him.

Receiving guidance is a lot easier than many people realise. We all receive guidance all the time. 'Life' is communicating with us always and all-ways, which makes sense if you think about the interconnectedness of all things. Receiving guidance is about paying exquisite attention to your life internally and externally — clouds, nature, what other people say, books, television, radio and to what arises within you, your thoughts, insights and feelings. We just need to notice the signs.

Have you had any of the following experiences yourself?

Someone you haven't seen for several years pops into your head, and then you bump into them. The phone rings and you instinctively know who it is. Someone recommends a book or a workshop to you and then so does someone else, and then a third person — perhaps it's time to get that book or attend that workshop.

Guidance is all around us. We simply need to notice the signs and listen — and to do this we need to be in the present.

So where to start? This chapter gives an overview of some of the many different ways we can receive guidance. We then explore the key ones in more depth in subsequent chapters

## *Listening to your intuition*

Listen to your intuition (in-tuition, inner tuition) at every opportunity. Ask it to tell you who you will be meeting today, what your lessons are likely to be, where you will find a parking space, what food you should eat for your highest good, which people you should spend time with and so on. Let your intuition know that you want its help now, and it will respond.

One of the most common questions I am asked is, How do I identify what is my imagination or wishful thinking and what is guidance? It does take time and practice. It is only through our experience of receiving guidance and then the benefit of hindsight that we can start to recognise for ourselves the characteristics of higher-level guidance.

Some insights will come through as absolute knowing. You won't know how you know, but you will know that you know.

One of the earliest occasions this happened for me was in a private consultation, when a woman asked me about her daughter. I saw clairvoyantly that her daughter had almost died when she was two years old. The woman, a sceptic, wanted me to tell her what she had nearly died of, and immediately I *knew* the daughter had suffered from a twisted colon. I didn't know *how* I knew, but I would have staked my life on it. It came straight out of my mouth and, sure enough, it was correct. This kind of *knowing* seems almost to bypass our rational-thinking left brain.

## *Spirit-world guides*

Guidance can also come from our loved ones in the spirit world. Receiving guidance from the spirit world is very different from receiving your own guidance. By all means listen to what your loved ones in the spirit world have to say, but if you would not take their advice when they were here, do not take it just because they are dead!

Loved ones in the spirit world can have their own agenda. They may want you to stay in the family business or in a destructive marriage because it is what *they* would do if they were here. This is *your* life and these are *your* decisions. Remember that. They can give you guidance only, and that is why they are called guides!

Your decisions should be based on all the information you have access to — past experience, knowledge, intellect, feelings, advisers and, if you like, what your guides say. You will find more about the mechanics of how to communicate with your guides in Chapter 8.

## *Higher-level guides*

As well as having spirit-world guides we also have higher-level guides. The higher-level guides are much better placed to help than lower-level guides, because they exist on a higher plane of consciousness and can see more of the whole picture.

I usually sense higher-level guides simply as loving energy and light, rather than with a physical form or name I can identify. They are wise, compassionate beings and often answer our questions with another question, one that makes us think about the real issue. They encourage us to make our own decisions and, in my experience, they have never told me what to do. They simply remind you of what you already know. They never criticise, but they are honest, allowing you the space to be your own worst critic and then helping you to reach a healthier perspective on what needs to happen.

When talking with guides, be they loved ones in the spirit world or higher beings, we need to be able to put the chatter in our heads to one side, or at least to slow it down, to listen to what is being said. Meditation is invaluable here. If you are serious about getting clear guidance, you need to learn to meditate. I have found Buddhist meditation classes very good and there are lots of others around too. The aim is to observe the mind and, through doing so, access the real you.

## *Pendulums*

Pendulums can be useful to reach 'yes' or 'no' answers on particular issues. Pendulums are usually made of wood, metal or crystal. It is a good idea to try them out before you buy one, to ensure you get one that works well and feels right for you. You may even find you already have a pendant that will work as a pendulum. Anything will do, provided it is equally weighted. I have seen some psychics use a wedding ring on a fine chain or strong thread with good results.

First, the pendulum needs to be 'programmed' to help you to tap into your own higher guidance. Hold it in your hands and think of this intention. Then, holding the pendulum cord or chain between your thumb and first finger, let the cord or chain fall over your first and middle fingers. This minimises the likelihood of you moving the pendulum by mistake yourself. You may find that resting your elbow on a flat surface, such as a table, helps you to get a clear signal. Find what works for you.

Now you need to get the pendulum to give you a signal/movement for 'Yes'. Intend* 'Give me a signal for yes', and watch what happens. The movement is usually a straight

---

* 'Intending' is stronger than asking but not as strong as commanding. The clearer your intent, the clearer you will find the movement of the pendulum.

line or a circle. If it moves in a circle, note whether its motion is clockwise or anticlockwise. Intend 'Give me a signal for no' and again watch what happens. The 'no' signal should be different from the one for 'yes'. If it isn't you will need to start all over again.

Once you have two different signals, it is time to put the pendulum to the test. Close your eyes and ask the pendulum 'Am I male/female?' (whichever one you are). Wait a few moments and then open your eyes to see the result. If it is correct, ask it other questions that you know the answers to.

When your pendulum has given you a succession of correct answers, you can move on to ask it questions you do not know the answers to. Pendulums can be particularly useful for finding things. Hold the pendulum over a map or diagram of the area in which you think you lost the item. Intend that the pendulum shows you where the missing item is. Then, hold the pendulum over each section of the map/diagram in turn, noting the different movements as you move.

If you have a problem getting your pendulum to move, try using your left hand and make sure you are relaxed. The secret is to not try too hard. I have known people to get hooked on their pendulums and not make any decisions without them. They are a tool, and do not replace listening with the whole of your being. In any case, chances are there will be times where you will need much more than a yes/no response.

## *Dreams*

Throughout humankind's history there have been stories about how dreams have been used to guide individuals and groups. There are several references in the Bible alone. In the early stages of my journey, I used dreams a lot to tell me what I most needed to know. The technique is quite simple, although I often had to ask on three consecutive nights before I received an answer I could make sense of. Don't be put off if you don't receive a message the very first night.

Write down that you would like a dream to guide you about X (the question you would like an answer to). It is important to be as specific as possible in your request. Then intend that you remember the dream, and put the piece of paper under your pillow. Leave a pen and paper at the side of your bed. As you go to sleep, imagine you are going to meet your guide or angel, and that you are taking the piece of paper with the question on it with you.

When you wake up, lie perfectly still and recall as much as you can about the dream. If you move you will cause a chunk of the dream to be lost. When you have remembered as much as possible, it is okay to move and write it down. Don't worry if you can't interpret it straight away.

Personally, I have found that the best way to interpret a dream is to look at the *feelings* arising within the dream. How did I feel when I saw X? How did I feel when Y happened? Then overlay the messages from the dream onto your life. For example, in one dream I found that I was a helicopter pilot. I was nervous about flying the helicopter for the first time without my instructor. I knew I was being tested, but although I was quite nervous, I knew I had it within me to pass the test. When I reviewed my dream journal some time later I realised that this particular dream had come through just before I did my first mediumship show in New Zealand, and the feelings I experienced in the dream corresponded with my feelings at that time.

Do you ever dream you are teaching, learning or being tested? Very often, what we face here in the physical reality comes through first in our dreams. Noticing our dreams helps us recognise our lessons when they happen and, when we see them as such, we are able to take them less personally and so move through them more easily.

It is a really good idea to keep a dream journal so you can look back on your dreams from time to time. You will be amazed at how much sense they make. Vivid dreams are especially important.

Dreams of vehicles seem to be particularly frequent for me. Perhaps they are for you too. Dreams of vehicles often indicate how we are doing on our journey, with the vehicle often representing our physical body.

A couple of dreams involving very different kinds of vehicles spring to mind. In one dream I was on the top deck of a double-decker bus. I did not know who was driving and there were a few other passengers on the bus. The bus was dirty, with litter strewn down the aisle. As the bus took corners I was thrown from side to side, but at no time did I feel unsafe. At that time in my life I had no direction or focus, no internal discipline or internal housekeeping to remove unwanted spirits. My life was a roller coaster emotionally and

I was literally swinging from side to side. The dream gave me a wake-up call to look at who I had with me on the spiritual levels. It motivated me to take charge of my life and take responsibility for keeping my internal space clear.

In another, more recent, dream I was in a shiny new Ferrari, driving confidently at speed. I wanted to share what I was experiencing with one of my family members, and in the dream let the family member sit in the car with me as a passenger. After a short while I realised that they weren't experiencing what I was because they weren't driving. I realised that what I needed to do was give them their own keys to their own Ferrari.

The dream showed me that it was better to let my family find their own success, their own way of living, and for me not to carry them as passengers, as there were better ways for me to help them.

Think about dreams you have had. Can you recall any specifically involving vehicles? Think about what was happening in your life at that time. Notice the vehicle. What kind of vehicle was it? What state of repair was it in? Were you driving, or was someone else? How were you driving? How did you feel in the vehicle? If you were driving too fast, were you trying to do too much in real life? If someone else was driving, were you letting someone else run your life rather than making your own decisions?

I have found it useful over the years to keep a dream journal because sometimes you just don't understand the dream at the time. Often I have found that weeks or even months later I have looked back at the dream and it makes perfect sense.

Dreams only ever give us so much information though, and at some stage you are going to want clearer, more specific or immediate guidance. In these cases meditation is the best way I know. It helps to be familiar with how to meditate because, at the times we most need it, we are likely to be so tense, stressed and emotional that it is hard to relax, let alone meditate. Practising at less stressful times is time well spent, and has the added advantage of leaving you in a good space for the rest of the day.

## *The quiet voice*

My 'best' advice has come from a calm, quiet voice within that I am usually only able to access after observing all the other different voices in my head, and letting them tire of me observing them. The calm, quiet voice says very little, but is always very profound. It is worth taking time to connect with yours. The first time it took me three days, but it was really worth it. You won't want to listen to any other voice.

The quiet voice is not a whisper; it is a clear voice that sounds as though it comes from a long way away. It often cannot be heard above the chatter of the other voices.

To connect with your quiet voice, first hold a clear intention that you wish to listen to your quiet voice about X. Sit in a meditative state, with your spine erect and your body relaxed, and observe all the other voices and feelings that arise within you. From time to time, re-state your intent to listen only to your quiet voice. It is worth persevering — I don't suggest sitting for long periods of time, but it is a good idea to make it your focus on successive days while meditating.

## *Channelling*

For me, channelling is very similar to listening to the spirit world, except I hold the clear intent of communicating with a higher-level guide about a particular issue, and I hold a higher vibration within my being, achieved through fasting, deep meditation, prayer and practice.

Here are some examples of things I have channelled. The wisdom they contain applies not only to me, or what was happening in my life, but can be used by almost anyone. See if they resonate with you.

### Channelling September 1997

I was reflecting on my dharmic* responsibilities as a child, as a sibling and as a partner. I realised that, more than anything, I am here to help others awaken and progress on their spiritual path. Within me I could feel a conflict with another part of me that just wanted to be, and in allowing myself to feel this conflict, the following words sprang forth.

> *In allowing myself to be, I allow myself to be love.*
> *Instead of pushing energy out to help people,*
> *I can allow myself to be, and more energy*
> *will flow through me. I allow myself to be fully*
> *present as a giver and receiver of love. I accept*
> *myself as I am right now. I love myself as I am*
> *right now.*
>
> *I am God, I am with God. All is God. Trust in*
> *God. Live in God. Live in love. Focus entirely on*

* Dharma is an Indian word meaning conscious right action.

*giving and receiving love. Do not allow yourself to be distracted by the imaginings of the monkey mind. Giving and receiving love is what you are here for. Giving and receiving love allows you to grow, to expand. It is the surest way of achieving spiritual growth. Focus on giving and receiving love. It does not matter what work you do — how you do what you do is more important.*

*Love your work, whatever you do, love all, serve all. When your love is limitless, so your growth will be limitless. By understanding the nature of your being all can be understood. You are pure energy. Explore the nature of energy. Energy cannot be created or destroyed. It can only change form; for example, from negative to positive.*

*Imagine a negative, depressed person transforming their energy to become a positive person. The potential is tremendous. So how do you change the negative to the positive?*

*Beyond the thought level: food — we are what we eat.*

*Inspirational, vibrant, alive, health-giving food; food with life force still in it.*

*Think positive, uplifting, inspiring thoughts.*

*You don't have to do anything. You are striving to do something worthwhile, something to enable you to value yourself. You are already loved and valued more than you can imagine.*

*Allow yourself to be at peace. There is no end to the amount of red herrings your ego will give you about the path to enlightenment. There is nowhere to go, there is no one thing you must do, no one-more book you must read, no one-more thing you must think about. You already are all that you want to be. Believe it, and know it to be true.*

*The universe is perfect, you are doing exactly the right thing, right now. How could you not? You are perfection itself.*

*Learning. Yes, you are here to learn, but also to remember, and to put into practice what you already know. The knowledge lies within. How much energy you expend looking for answers outside of yourself, when most of this knowledge you already know. Look within, still the mind, free your senses from the illusory world. Control your senses, master your senses. They will serve you well. Too often it is the other way around; with you serving your senses.*

*As we approach a time of great evolutionary change, individuals have great opportunity for growth. The rate of change is set to accelerate still further.* God, God, God, God, Love, Love, Love, Love, Love. *Notice how this stills the mind. It settles it to receive kind words.* Live in love. Live in God.

*Some concepts take time to assimilate, so be*

*gentle with yourself. Be gentle with all things for this is the nature of the Divine.*

## Channelling, September 1997

*'How can my life be a better expression of the love that I am?' By finding peace within yourself.*
*'How do I do that?' By allowing yourself to be.*
*'What do I need to do to allow myself to be?'*
*Let go.*
*'Let go?' Let go of all that you think you know, what is right or wrong, what is good or bad.*
*'How will I know when I have let go?' You will be free.*
*'Why do I worry?' Fear.*
*'Fear?' Fear of being unworthy, having to do something to be worthy. Just by being, you do what you came here to do, opening to love/light. It is only the ego that says it has to do certain things. Nothing is required of you.*
*Can you love yourself knowing that nothing is required of you, that you already are all that you need to be?*

# CHAPTER 7

# RELAXATION, VISUALISATION AND MEDITATION

Relaxation, visualisation and meditation are all useful tools to help us better understand who we are. Sometimes the boundaries between each get a little blurred, but briefly:

*relaxation* is learning to relax your physical body;

*visualisation* is using the mind to create a certain state within you; and

*meditation* is about accessing the true you.

In the exercises that follow you will get to experience each in turn, starting with relaxation, so you can understand the difference for yourself. You will note that the wording of some of the exercises is used again and again. This is deliberate. As the words start to become familiar to you, you will find yourself beginning to relax. Repetition also makes it easier for you to learn the process, so you can repeat it yourself whenever you wish without having to read the words out of the book.

# EXERCISE: Relaxation
## Experience

Allow yourself an uninterrupted period of time, at least 20 minutes, to experience relaxation. Decide before you start how long you will allow. Make sure that you will not be disturbed. You may want to play some relaxing music or burn aromatic oils to help you relax.

Sit or lie in a position that is comfortable for you. Let your awareness move down into your toes and, as you breathe out, imagine that you are breathing out all the tension stored in your toes. Just breathe it out and let it go. Allow your toes to relax more deeply than they ever have before. When your toes are completely relaxed, let your awareness move slowly into the rest of your feet.

Using your breath as a focus, imagine that you are breathing out all the tension stored in your feet. Just breathe it out and let it go. Allow your feet to relax more deeply than they ever have before. When your feet are completely relaxed, let your awareness move slowly into your ankles.

Notice how your ankles are feeling and, as you breathe out, imagine that you are breathing out all the tension stored in your ankles. Just breathe it out and let it go. Allow your ankles to relax more deeply than they ever have before. When your ankles are completely relaxed, completely at peace, let your awareness move into your lower legs.

Notice how this process of relaxing each part of the body in turn is already helping your lower legs to relax; it's as if they already know what to do. With every 'out' breath the tension in your lower legs is releasing and dissolving. With each and every breath your lower legs are becoming more and more relaxed and, effortlessly now, your awareness moves into your knees.

You notice the tension that your knees are holding is already starting to release as, with each breath out, you breathe out tension. With each breath out you simply let go. Even your upper legs are starting to relax now as the feeling of relaxation starts to spread through your body. Every breath out releases tension from your upper legs, every breath out takes you into a deeper state of peace and relaxation. And so your awareness moves gently and peacefully into your hips and pelvic area. You can feel the tension getting ready to release, and again with every breath out all the tension is released. Again, with every breath out your cells learn to let go.

The cells of your body are letting go at a deeper level than they ever have done before. It is as though each part of your body in turn is learning from the parts that have gone before, and each part is becoming more relaxed as you gently and peacefully relax each part of your body in turn. Soon the whole of your pelvic area is relaxed, more relaxed than it has ever been before.

You notice that the feeling of deep relaxation is making its way into your stomach and lower back. Every cell is giving up its tension to the out breath effortlessly and easily. Every cell is becoming even more relaxed than it ever was before.

And so the feeling of deep relaxation goes on moving up into your chest and upper back. Every breath is helping you release the tension; every breath is helping you to feel even more relaxed. Even your shoulders are starting to soften now as the feeling of deep relaxation starts moving into them. Every breath is breathing out more tension; every breath is helping you feel more and more relaxed. Allow yourself to breathe deeply now and really let your shoulders relax at a deep level. Every breath is breathing out tension; every breath is making you feel more relaxed and more at peace.

As your shoulders allow themselves to relax completely, notice how that relaxed feeling is flowing down your arms and into your hands. With every breath you are breathing out tension stored in the arms and the hands. With every breath you are feeling more and more relaxed. And that lovely relaxed feeling is flowing effortlessly and freely into your neck and throat areas. With every breath the cells of your neck and throat are feeling more relaxed, more at peace.

This feeling of deep relaxation is almost throughout you now. So many parts of your body have allowed themselves to relax at a deep level that the remaining parts are already starting to do the same. You can feel your ears and your eyes relaxing now. You can feel all the muscles of your face relaxing.

It takes so much energy to hold onto tension and now you can simply breathe it out and let it go. Let all the tension that is stored in your head and face go. Allow all the cells of your body to relax at a deep level. Allow all your being to remember what it is to be relaxed and at peace.

You can't help but notice that every breath now is taking you deeper and deeper into a state of relaxation, deeper and deeper into the most peaceful state you have ever experienced. And every breath allows you to relax ever more deeply, more deeply than you ever imagined possible. And as you allow yourself to be completely relaxed, completely at peace, you realise that with every breath your sense of relaxation is becoming deeper than you ever imagined possible.

Allow yourself to rest in this fully relaxed and peaceful state for as long as you feel your body needs and, when you are ready, let your awareness start to come back to the day. Know that as you let your awareness return, your cells will bring with them the memory and the knowledge of this deeply relaxed state, and that at any time ❱

in the future you will be able to access this deeply relaxed state simply by using your breath as a focus.

Know that each time you allow your body to relax in this way the process of relaxing will become easier and easier, and the state of peace and relaxation will become deeper and deeper. In no time at all you will be able to access profound and deep states of relaxation and peacefulness at will.

## Reflection

Reflect on how this experience of relaxation felt for you.

What happened? What helped you to relax and what didn't? What were the key differences in how you felt during this exercise and how you usually feel?

## Understanding

So why do we feel so different when we relax?

Like all animals, we have a *fight or flight* response. When we are under stress our physical bodies get ready to literally fight off an attacker or to run away. Blood rushes to the major muscle groups, to our arms to fight and to our legs to run. In doing this it is taken from other parts of the body, including organs. Adrenalin starts pumping and we may feel our heart pounding in our chest. Our digestive system slows down or stops, and our bowels and bladder may empty. When the stress is over, noradrenalin kicks in and our body functions start returning to normal.

So what causes stress? Stress is caused by anything that is not as you would like it to be; in other words, anything that you are resisting. When I studied stress as a training manager for Lloyds Bank I found that there are two kind of stress: *acute* stress and *chronic* stress.

Acute stress is when something suddenly happens, like an accident, or losing your job. Chronic stress develops over a long period, like a large mortgage or having an elderly relative stay with you. Of the two, chronic stress is the most damaging because it causes our bodies to be in a perpetual state of fight or flight.

Sometimes the stressful situation goes on for so long that we no longer recognise that we are stressed. We get used to how we are and forget that we used to feel differently. We no longer recognise how much tension our bodies are holding onto until we experience again how it feels to be relaxed. Have you ever gone away on holiday and found that you couldn't unwind and relax until several days into the holiday? This is likely to be a sign that your body is in a fight or flight state and that you are under stress.

When the body is relaxed, the cells no longer hold on to tension or energy and the consciousness in the cells no longer resists. In a relaxed state, the cells of the body have a remarkable ability to repair themselves and communicate with each other so healing can take place. We find ourselves thinking clearly and we are more likely to see things as they are.

In noticing what relaxed feels like in this exercise you are better placed to notice the times that you are anything other than relaxed. With this knowledge of how to relax you can be more in control of how your body feels and functions.

## Planning your next step

What would you do differently next time to help you relax better? When will you next allow yourself time to relax? How long will you allow yourself to relax for?

Relaxation exercises such as the one above are often used in an abbreviated form to help begin either a guided visualisation or a meditation. They help you relax your body and your mind. They help the mind relax by giving it something to do, such as observing the breath or focusing on a particular part of the body.

Relaxation exercises are also useful if you are having trouble getting to sleep, or if you need healing. Often I will use a relaxation technique such as the one above to help my clients relax before they receive a healing. When your physical body is completely relaxed the cells of your body are more open to receiving healing energy because there is little or no resistance.

### EXERCISE: Guided visualisation to release worries

Guided visualisations are used to help create a particular state within you, or perhaps to help you see a situation in a different way. I have used guided visualisations for many different purposes over the years. A couple of examples that I have found particularly useful are given below. In time, you may find that you wish to create your own visualisations, to address your own individual needs.

### Experience

Sit comfortably and allow yourself to relax. When you are ready, let your awareness move to your breathing. Notice your breath. You are not trying to change it in any way, you are simply noticing it. Let it be.

Allow yourself to pay exquisite attention to your breath, the in breath and the out breath.

Allow yourself to breathe.

All that is important right now is your breath.

If you find your mind wandering, bring it gently but firmly back to the breath.

Observe the breath, noticing how it feels.

The in breath and the out breath.

Your breath is All That Is important right now.

Soon we will be using a guided visualisation to help you release any worries you may be holding on to, but for now just notice your breath. It is All That Is important right now.

Observe your breath, feel how it feels.

When you are ready, imagine that in your hands you are holding two large glasses. Imagine that you can feel the glasses resting comfortably in your hands. Notice how they feel. Notice the diameter of the glasses, and how the surface of the glasses feels.

These glasses represent fears and worries that you are still holding onto in some way. Notice how they feel. Are they heavy or light? Notice what is in each of the glasses. Are they a particular colour? How do you feel about what is in the glasses?

Notice how full and heavy each of them is. Is one of the glasses heavier than the other? Do they change as you look at them?

These glasses represent the different worries that you are currently holding onto. In your right hand are the logical, rational worries that you may well be conscious of.

How would it be to put that glass down?

Try it now. Notice what happens.

How would it be to put down the glass in your left hand?

Again, try it now, and notice what happens.

Let your awareness move to your sacral centre, an energy ❱

centre about two inches below your navel. It is through the sacral centre that we process deep-seated emotions. Imagine a ball of light energy forming around your sacral area. Instinctively, you know that you are able to give freely from this centre, because it is always replenished for you. Imagine giving from this centre to all the people and demands in your life, and knowing that you can give freely because always the energy is replenished from within.

Notice how it feels.

Now try putting the glass in your right hand down again while you also focus on giving. Your main awareness should be on giving.

How does it feel this time? Are you happy to put the glass down and leave it there?

Now let your awareness move to your left hand. The left glass represents irrational, often unconscious fears and worries you are holding onto. Again, let your main focus be on the giving you are doing from the self-replenishing ball of light energy that has now expanded to incorporate your solar plexus energy centre, situated at the base of your breastbone.

As you give from this ball of light, thinking about all the different ways in which you can give to people and help people, let yourself put down the glass in your left hand.

Can you put it down and leave it there?

When you are ready, allow your consciousness to return to the here and now. Feeling your body, your fingers and your toes, your arms and your legs. You may want to move your fingers and your toes before opening your eyes.

### Reflection

What happened? How do you feel about what happened?

## Understanding

People get different results with this exercise. Some can put down both glasses first time and some take longer. Everyone benefits, though, from an increased awareness of what they are holding onto and why. Feel free to do this exercise as often as you need to.

## Planning your next step

Would it be useful for you to do this exercise again? If so, when?

# EXERCISE: Guided visualisation to heal yourself
## Experience

Use the relaxation process given at the start of this chapter to relax each part of your body in turn. When the whole of your physical body is relaxed, allow your awareness to move into the part of your body that needs healing. Just be with that part, here and now.

You are not judging this part in any way; you are just being present with it.

Feel the flow of energy in the part of the body that is affected, and be open to insights and understandings about the nature of the condition. Send thanks to the part of the body affected for all that it does for you. Feel love and healing flowing to the part, for as long as you feel the need.

Then, when you are ready, gently let your awareness return to the whole of your physical body, and then back to your environment. You may want to move your fingers and your toes before opening your eyes. When you are ready, open your eyes.

## Reflection

What happened? How did you feel? How does the part that received the healing now feel?

## Understanding

Why are guided visualisations so useful? Our minds and bodies are inextricably intertwined. When we think something, our body has no way of telling if what we are thinking is true, so it responds in a way that is appropriate to what is running through our head. If we imagine ourselves on a sunny peaceful beach, our body will start responding to that, and if we imagine sitting in rush-hour traffic, our body will respond to that too.

Imagine a scene where two people are walking across a road. One is listening to music on a Walkman. Suddenly there is a screech of brakes, and a car nearly hits them both from behind. The one wearing the Walkman is completely oblivious to what nearly happened; the other is completely shook up by it. The two are in the same situation, but there are two very different physical, emotional and mental responses because they are experiencing that same situation very differently.

So, even when the situation we are in is very stressful, if we give our mind something else to do we can create much more resourceful states in our bodies, and reduce the damage that the fight or flight responses can do.

## Planning your next step

How could you modify the above guided visualisation to make it more effective for you? When will you try out the new visualisation?

Meditation is also a useful way to help us experience moments of complete awareness, where we can connect with all that we are and All That Is. The only place where we can possibly find out who we are is in the 'now'. If you are thinking about the past or the present you are in your mind, but we have already seen that you are more than mind. To find our true selves we have to go beyond mind.

I find it much easier to meditate in the early morning, when the world is still, than I do at other times. Many people find it best to have some kind of routine to their meditation practice, such as always meditating in the same chair, or in the same place, or at the same time, or to the same music. Burning incense or an aromatic oil may also help, as our sense of smell has a particular ability to help take us straight back to a place, a time or even a state of being.

You may want to use the relaxation exercise at the start of this chapter to relax your mind and body before moving on to each of the following meditations.

As always make sure that you will not be disturbed. When you are ready to begin, sit in a comfortable position with your back straight and your head and shoulders relaxed. Your shoulders should be in alignment with your ears, and your hips in alignment with your shoulders.

### EXERCISE: Candle flame meditation

When you are ready, light a candle, and take a few moments to observe your breathing and relax your body. Observe the candle. Notice everything about it. As you watch the candle flame, allow ❯

the whole of your body to relax. As you watch the candle flame, allow your mind to relax.

When you are ready to take the relaxation deeper, take in a breath and, as you do so, imagine that you are taking in the light of the candle flame. Hold the sense of the candle flame as a focus for as long as you can.

When the sense of the candle flame fades, or when you are ready to return to present-moment awareness, let your awareness come back to how your body feels. You may want to move your fingers and your toes before opening your eyes.

## EXERCISE: Count of four meditation

When you are ready, let your awareness go to your breathing. Notice the movement of the breath as it enters and leaves your body. Allow your awareness to focus either on the movement of the lungs or the movement of air coming in through your nose or mouth.

Count each in breath — one, two ... If you find your attention wandering gently but firmly bring it back to the breath and resume your counting from one again. Each time you wander off into mind, simply notice that this has happened, and be thankful that you are fully present again. Resume your counting from one. Continue with this practice for as long as you like.

## Exercise: God/Love meditation

Notice your breathing; really notice how it feels to breathe. You don't have to change your breathing in any way, just observe it. Breathe in and breathe out. Notice how your body is feeling. If there are any pockets of tension breathe them out, let them go. Really let yourself relax.

Let your attention rest in your heart centre, in the middle of your chest. As you hold your focus there say to yourself God, God, God, (or Love, Love, Love) repeatedly. Notice how this starts to soften your heart centre.

Your mind will try to distract you — each time you notice you have drifted off somewhere else, just bring your attention, gently but firmly, back to your heart centre and repeat again God, God, God. Sit doing this for as long as you wish.

When you return from the meditation, sit quietly for a few moments before moving about.

You can also use the words God and Love as a mantra, something you repeat throughout the day to keep you focused in the now.

## Reflection

What happened for you during each of the meditations? Which of the three meditations did you prefer? Why?

## Understanding

Some people find it easier to meditate when there is something visual to focus on. Some prefer focusing on something physical, and some prefer using sound as a focus. The three meditations are designed to help you find which is the best kind for you. A is mostly visual, B is mostly feeling orientated and C is mainly sound. When beginning to meditate most people find listening to a voice useful as this gives the mind something to do while the body is relaxing. When you become more experienced, you may find that silent meditation is best for you.

It is always a good idea to relax the body as a first stage to meditation. You can do this through physical exercise such as yoga or t'ai chi, or by taking a bath or a shower. You may just want to use the relaxation exercise in this chapter. If you do, feel free to adapt it in a way that works best for you. By relaxing our body we automatically start to help the mind to relax, making it easier for us to experience our true nature.

You will find that, by putting aside time each day to meditate and connect with your true nature, you automatically start having more moments where you experience your true nature in day-to-day life.

## EXERCISE: Mindfulness meditation

This is a different kind of meditation practice that I have found very useful. It is done with your eyes open and you can do as much or as little of it as you wish. Mindfulness meditation is the kind of meditation that can be done at any time of day. No matter how busy your life is, you can always make time for it.

Mindfulness meditation is the practice of exquisite present-moment awareness.

The next time you are doing something mundane such as washing the dishes, brushing your teeth or simply walking, start paying exquisite attention to all that you are experiencing. Notice everything that is happening, in the smallest detail — the sound of the water running, the fragrance of the suds and how they affect the back of your nose, the warmth of the water on your skin, the small cut on your finger you had forgotten about, the way the suds slide off the dishes, the sound of the suds popping. Notice absolutely everything. Give the act of dishwashing your fullest attention. Be completely and fully present as you carry out each action.

## Reflection

How did it feel to be fully present while doing something mundane? How did you feel about the task? How often are you fully present? How often are you doing things mindlessly?

## Understanding

For my first mindful meditation I chose washing the dishes, a part of housework that I don't mind too much. It gave me an incredible insight into why I have never liked housework.

Washing dishes while I was fully conscious was completely different from what I had experienced before. I marvelled at the bubbles and the water and how the dishes sparkled after washing, something I hadn't done before, or at least not since I was a child. I understood with a jolt why my kids so love washing up. They are five and seven and still wonder at the bubbles. To them washing dishes is play, not a chore. I wondered if that was why we must become as children to enter the kingdom of God.

I thought about how housework was really a bore and a drudgery to me, and I realised that it was because I was not doing it mindfully. All the time I did the housework, in fact before I even started, I was moaning to myself about having to do it. I was thinking about all the other things I could do that were more enjoyable. I was thinking about how it was stopping me from spending time with my kids. It soon became clear that I resented having to do housework, really resented it. I needed a maid or a cleaner, someone to do all that awful work for me. And so it went on. The voices in my head were › well rehearsed and knew just how to push my buttons.

Through mindfulness meditation I realised that it was not the housework that was the problem. It was what was happening in my head *while* I did the housework. Housework really isn't that terrible; there are certainly far worse things in life. It was *me* who was making it so much worse than it was.

So I turned the situation on its head. When I do housework nowadays I am mindful. The voices are still there, but I see one of my best meditation practices being to enjoy the housework, enjoy being fully here and now. I also notice the voices in my head and all they do to try and take me out of the present moment and into mind. The voices are still there, but they do not stop me from enjoying the now — unless I let them.

### Planning your next step

You know yourself better than anyone else does. What kind of meditation practice would be most likely to work for you? Would you prefer to join a group, meditate with a friend or be by yourself? When? For how long?

How are you most likely to sabotage your own plans to meditate, and what can you do to prevent that from happening?

# CHAPTER 8

# GUIDES

People often ask me how I do what I do. I do have a natural ability as many, if not all, of us have but it has also taken a lot of practice and a lot of mindfulness.

Initially, I practised receiving guidance for myself, and then for close friends and family members. It was some time before I had the confidence to practise giving messages in a group. This is a whole different experience and requires an additional set of skills.

In this book I am focusing on what it is like to communicate with the spirit world one to one. The more advanced mediumship guidance will form part of a further book, exclusively on mediumship.

This chapter is very much a 'beginner's guide' on how to start communicating with your spirit-world guides.

Spirit-world guides are around us all the time — they are simply on a different frequency to us. Signals from a local television or radio station could be going through the room where you sit but you will be completely oblivious to them without the necessary piece of equipment, tuned to the right frequency, to receive the signals. In the same way, the spirit world is communicating with us all the time. All that happened to me 11 years ago was that somehow I learned to tune into the spirit-world frequencies.

Very often, it isn't that we don't have the right piece of equipment to hear spirit-world guides — we just haven't been trained how to use it. So, if you are serious about being able to see, hear and sense the spirit world, the rest of this chapter will help you to get started. It is easier than most people think.

First, make sure you are relaxed, comfortable, alert and not tired. You also need to be in good spirits, so to speak — not depressed or stressed.

In my experience, it is also important not to have taken alcohol or drugs of any kind before attempting this exercise. Alcohol can open us up psychically but can leave us without a control mechanism. If you attract a troublesome spirit you may find that you can't get rid of it because of the effect of the alcohol. Some drugs may affect us in a similar way so, to be on the safe side, it is best to avoid both alcohol and drugs.

You may choose to have someone with you or you can do this exercise on your own, whichever feels most comfortable to you.

## *Protection*

First, a few words about protection. You may have heard about the need to protect yourself before doing spiritual work. It is good practice to ask for protection before doing any kind of spiritual work — ask God, your guides, your angels, whatever feels right for you. You can also imagine surrounding and filling yourself with love and light. I have found that white light is particularly good for protection, and so is gold light.

Protection simply means that negative energies or spirits will not be able to affect you. Reiki symbols can also be used to bless a room or a space, or you can smudge the room using white sage. (Reiki is a form of natural healing that uses symbols that can also be used to cleanse and raise the vibration of a person or place. White sage is dried sage, traditionally used by Native American peoples to cleanse a person or place.)

Problems usually occur with spirit communication only when the person here is depressed, tired, has been drinking or taking drugs and/or is using a Ouija-board or automatic handwriting to communicate with spirits.

Generally speaking, spirits want to talk with us for good reasons, but like attracts like. If the receiver is not in a good place energetically, mentally or emotionally, they will connect with spirits/energies that similarly are not in a good place.

Initially, it may be a good idea to make contact with one of your guides and the following is a useful exercise to make that first contact. You may find it useful to record this passage onto a tape to begin with. Pre-recorded tapes and CDs are also available from my website *www.jeanettewilson.com*.

### EXERCISE: Contacting your guide

Do not attempt to communicate with the spirit world if you are emotionally upset or have taken alcohol or drugs, as you may not have the level of control to make a safe and loving connection.

First, make sure you have sufficient time for this exercise. You may be sitting for anything up to 30 minutes. Make sure you will not be disturbed and that you are dressed comfortably, in loose-fitting clothes. Tight clothes can restrict the flow of energy.

When you are ready to begin, start by sitting comfortably with your spine erect. This is important to ensure a free flow of energy up and down your spine. Close your eyes and take a few deep breaths. Really pay attention to your breathing. Notice how it feels. Are you breathing from the top of your lungs or the bottom, or both? Don't try to change your breathing in any way, just notice it.

As you breathe, notice that you are also in a physical body. Notice how your physical body feels. Feel your feet on the floor, feel the chair or ground beneath you, feel your fingers and your toes. Feel your shoulders, your neck and your head. Feel yourself in the whole of your body at once.

Notice that within your body you can also sense yourself as energy, a frequency if you like. Notice *how* your energy feels. Notice how this energy that you are can extend beyond your physical form. You can feel the energy you are, around your body, as well as within it.

Feel your physical form and the energy that you are. Notice how they overlap and yet are different. Know that you are spirit as well as a physical form, and know that your spirit can transcend or move beyond your physical form, whenever you hold that intent.

Using your imagination, imagine that you can sense wise and loving spirit beings forming a circle around you. Imagine that you can see these wise and loving beings, and that you see them as beings of light.

All around you now are a circle of wise and loving light beings, standing just the right distance from you. Their presence helps you feel safe and protected and loved. These loving light beings want nothing from you. They are simply here to help you meet with your

GUIDES

guide. Allow yourself to feel the love that these light beings are sending you. Feel their love for you gently opening your heart centre in the middle of your chest. You don't need to do anything, just allow yourself to feel the love and light they are sending you.

These light beings love you unconditionally. They know all that you have been through, all the choices you have made and why you made them and they love you completely, exactly as you are.

Really let yourself feel the love that they have for you and, as you do so, allow yourself to become aware of a brighter light that is starting to approach the outside of the circle. This brighter light is one of your guides. Allow yourself to feel the unconditional love and light that your guide is sending to you. You might sense it as light, or as a feeling. Notice how your guide's higher and finer vibration is starting to merge with your own energy field. Notice how your own energy field is affected by this incoming stream of love and light. Your guide is coming close to the circle perimeter now, and increasingly you can feel love and light shooting towards you, into your space, into your energy field, raising your vibration and your consciousness still further.

Intend that your guide comes closer still. Allow yourself to feel the complete and total love your guide has for you. Notice that your guide has a gift for you. Accept the gift, giving thanks for it. You may want to ask why that particular gift. If so, telepathically send out a question to your guide. Why this? Notice their response.

What is it that your guide most wants to tell you? Be open to concepts and feelings as well as to words and pictures. What is it *you* most need to learn right now? Again, be open to all impressions, sensing for concepts and feelings, listening for words and looking for images.

Ask 'Are you the highest guide available to me at this time?' If the answer is 'No', ask them to help you connect with your highest guide. Intend to connect with your highest guide and ask the first guide to stand back while your highest guide comes through. You may find that the first guide, the one who then stands back, leaves you with a gift, usually an insight of some kind before leaving.

Spend time with your highest guide, just feeling their energy, their resonance. It is important to do this so you will recognise them again. Ask your guide to do what they can to assist you in getting a better connection with them. You may feel your energy shifting as they make the necessary adjustments.

Ask your guide if they have a name. Notice the response. Ask your guide 'What is it I most need to know or understand right now?' Again, notice the response.

When you are ready to let your awareness return to the physical dimension, thank your guide for all that they have done and thank the light beings for facilitating this communication. Let your awareness come back to the present gently. Feel yourself as energy, spirit. Feel your physical body, your arms and your legs, your fingers and your toes, and notice your breathing once more. You may want to move your fingers and your toes before opening your eyes.

Silently give thanks for this experience and know that each time you connect with your guides the connection will get stronger and clearer. Give yourself a pat on the back for taking this first step. Well done!

### Reflection
What happened? What are your feelings about what happened?

## Understanding

Our guides, and we can have many of them, are there to help guide us on our journey here. Sometimes you will find that the most prominent guide is a family member who has passed over. At other times they are people we have seemingly never met before. As a general rule it is best to always work with the highest guide that is available to you. There are some exceptions to this rule. For example, when I'm healing I work with a guide who has healing abilities or knows about the human body. I may even work with the patient's guides if that is more appropriate.

Don't be disappointed if you don't get a name at first. It was three years before I found out the names of two of my guides, and knowing their names has not made a jot of difference to my ability to receive guidance from them. The desire to know our guides' names seems to come mainly from our ego. Giving a guide a name can actually limit our understanding of who they are. It is more important to be able to sense *how* they feel so that you can recognise their particular resonance when they are around.

At different times you will find you get a better connection with your guides than at others. When you do get a particularly good connection, you may want to spend more time with that guide. It is also a good idea to recognise what it was you did differently to create a better connection. Were you more energised? Had you eaten something different? What were you doing or thinking about immediately before making a connection? What kind of day had you had?

You may want to spend a few sessions talking with your guides before moving on to talking with a loved one from the spirit world, or you may feel you want to do it straight away. Just trust your feelings.

> It is not uncommon for people to see a loved one in the spirit world during this first exercise of contacting a guide, as our loved ones often use any opportunity they can to get through and let us know they are alright. If this happened to you, don't be surprised if you later find out that the family member you saw isn't actually your highest guide. Your highest guide will just have stood to one side if they felt it was more appropriate for you to see a loved one first.
>
> Next time you try this exercise, if you see the same family member again ask them if they are the highest guide available to you. Usually we find that they are not. They want to help us but they aren't our highest guide. They then stand to one side and help us to connect with another guide, very often a Master Teacher guide from a higher dimension.

My main two guides are Ortan and Medoc. Ortan is the more advanced or senior guide who oversees my growth here — and Medoc, well, he tells me he is 'in training'. That had me worried for a while. I stand up in front of hundreds of people to pass on messages with a guide that is 'in training' himself — but that's another story!

Medoc is perfect for what he needs to do. In the same way that I have had no formal training in how to be a medium, Medoc has had no formal training either. Together we 'experiment' with what is possible. Neither of us is limited by how mediumship has been done before and each of us shares what we learn. I share my knowledge in books and at shows and Medoc shares his knowledge in the spiritual dimensions. Together we are adding to the knowledge that exists about mediumship. Our way may not be the best way but it is one that works for us.

Our guides can also help us to heal. If you are feeling in need of healing for a specific complaint or are just in need of a general boost, you may want to try this next exercise.

### EXERCISE: Receiving healing from your healing guide

This guided visualisation can take up to 30 minutes, or longer if you wish. As with the other exercises, make sure you will not be disturbed and that you are dressed comfortably in loose-fitting clothes. You can burn incense or an aromatic oil if you find that helps you to relax.

Before starting this visualisation it is important to be clear about what it is you want healing for, and to intend that you connect with the healing guide that can best assist you at this time. When you are ready to begin, settle yourself in a comfortable position. Lying down on a bed is probably best for this particular visualisation, as sometimes the sense of relaxation is so deep that you can easily drift off to sleep. If you do find this happening, do not be concerned as the healing still takes place, but at a deeper level.

Spend a few moments noticing your breath, not trying to change it in any way, just noticing it. Observe the in breath and the out breath. Use your breath as a focus to help you relax the rest of your body, starting from your toes and moving up. Take as long as you need. Let each part of your body relax in turn and do not move on to the next part until you can sense that the previous part is completely relaxed.

When you are feeling completely relaxed, imagine that you can ❱

sense wise and loving spirit beings forming a circle around you. Using your imagination, imagine that you can see these wise and loving beings and that you can see them as beings of light. As you look around you, using your internal vision you can see this circle of wise and loving light beings standing just the right distance from you. Their presence helps you to feel safe and protected and loved.

These loving light beings want nothing from you. They are simply here to help you receive a healing from one of your healing guides. Allow yourself to feel the love that these light beings are sending you. Feel their love for you gently opening your heart centre in the middle of your chest. You don't need to do anything, just allow yourself to feel the love and light they are sending you.

These light beings love you unconditionally. They know all that you have been through, all the choices you have made and why you made them, and they love you completely, exactly as you are.

Really let yourself feel the love they have for you and, as you do so, allow yourself to become aware of a brighter light that is starting to approach the outside of the circle. This is the light of the healing guide that can best help you at this time. Allow yourself to feel the unconditional love and light that your healing guide is sending to you. You might sense it as light, or as a feeling.

As your healing guide draws close, convey to them telepathically, using your mind, what it is you want healing for. Sense your guide's higher, finer healing vibration starting to reach the part or parts where you most need healing. Feel the higher, finer healing energies merging with your own energy field. Notice how your own energy field is affected by this incoming stream of healing energy. Imagine each and every cell being infused with divine healing energy. Notice how it feels.

GUIDES

Send love to the part/parts requiring healing, and send love to the healing guide. Almost immediately you will feel love and light coming back to you from the healing guide. Use this energy to help you to relax even more deeply. Notice how in this state of deep relaxation you can feel the divine healing rays even more profoundly.

Allow the healing to take place at a deep level, and let your awareness start to understand the reasons behind the condition you have. Allow yourself to understand how you may have contributed to the condition. Allow yourself to see, on a physical level, what you can do to heal yourself.

Spend as long as you need with your guide. You will know instinctively when the healing is complete. When you are ready, thank your healing guide telepathically for their love and healing. Thank the beings of light for their assistance too. Start feeling yourself back in your physical body once more. Feel your arms and your legs, your fingers and your toes. You may want to move your fingers and your toes before opening your eyes. You may want to lie with your eyes open for a few minutes before getting up from the bed.

## Reflection

How did you feel before the exercise? How did you feel during the exercise? How do you feel now?

## Understanding

Healing guides exist on the higher dimensions. Initially it can be quite difficult to perceive them, so this guided visualisation is a good way to start. In it you use your imagination to help create the experience. If you felt heat, tingling or spirit hands on your body ❯

during this exercise, well done! You have had your first tangible encounter with one of your healing guides.

## Planning your next step

Many conditions require more than one treatment. I ask for a healing myself each evening, just before sleep, and find I sleep more deeply as a result. If you enjoyed doing the exercise and found some benefit from it, you may want to schedule in some time during the next seven days to repeat it. Remember that each time you do this exercise your connection with your healing guide will become stronger and you will feel more benefit. Also, remember that healing of this nature should not take the place of conventional medicine. You should always seek the advice of a medically qualified doctor about any health conditions which are causing you concern.

The guides that work with me when I am healing seem to vary, and sometimes I find I end up working with the client's guides, as happened in this next story.

Alice came to see me because she was having a bit of trouble with a stiff right knee that was tending to give way on her at times. Alice was in her seventies, and was worried that her knee would give out as she crossed a road. Alice had thought long and hard about coming to see me because she had heard good reports, but wasn't really sure about what I did and whether it would work for her. As soon as I started to work I found that she had her son in the spirit world with her. He had taken his own life and really wanted to make amends. He asked me if he could help in his mother's healing.

His request put me in a bit of a spot. Not everyone who

comes for healing wants a message from the other side. You could really cause distress if you were to say something and the client didn't want a message. I decided to talk in general terms and see what kind of a reaction I got.

'Sometimes when I am doing the healing I sense spirit beings that are related to the person I am healing. If I happen to sense someone for you would you want me to say anything?'

'Ooh yes, I would. I didn't realise you did that too. But yes if it's not too much trouble, that would be lovely.'

'I do have a young man with you. He tells me he is your son and he is very, very sorry for what he did.'

Tears had already started to trickle down Alice's face, but she was smiling through them. 'Is he alright?' she asked eagerly.

'He's fine,' I said. Her son Stephen in the spirit world was feeling what she was feeling. The emotion had been held back a long time — over 30 years, he told me in my head.

'He is sorry he took his own life.' I knew she needed to know he had shown me this. Alice nodded and a few more tears rolled down her face. There hadn't been a day when she had not thought of him.

'Stephen has asked me if he can assist me healing your knee.'

Alice smiled. 'That would be lovely.'

I knelt to heal Alice's knee and allowed her son to come in very close. I could feel his energy mingling with my own, but he made no attempt to take over my thoughts as I had known other spirits to sometimes do. I was able to relax and to allow his energy to come through more fully. I knew absolutely that he posed no threat to me.

Stephen's energy was warm and kind and gentle. As we healed his mum together he told me about his life in the spiritual dimensions and I relayed everything he said. It was fascinating for both of us. Alice's son had regretted his action so much that on the spiritual side of life he now helped other people who had taken their own life. He worked mainly with younger men, particularly ones in their teenage years and early 20s. He had found he was naturally compassionate towards them because he knew first-hand what it was like to make such a decision. His work with others also helped him to find a new level of compassion and forgiveness towards himself.

Stephen's main passion, though, was healing. On the spiritual side he had found that he loved to heal. He was so much happier in the spirit world than he had been here. People were just not judgemental of him any more and he could just be himself. His fondest wish was that his mother would understand that he was happy.

Stephen very much regretted what he had done and the pain he had caused, but had come to realise that he couldn't turn the clock back and make things alright. He had to make the most of how things now were. I could see that he had grown so much since passing, and I think Alice saw that too.

All too soon I could feel the spiritual energies winding down and sensed the healing coming to a close. It was time for Stephen to go. Alice and Stephen said their goodbyes. When she came to leave Alice could not believe how good her knee felt.

'It's just like new,' she exclaimed. 'Thank you.'

'Don't thank *me*,' I said.

We both knew that this one had been down to Stephen.

My link with Stephen had been beautiful. He was easy to talk to and we worked well together. We had been brought together by his mother's pain and his heartfelt desire to do what he could to help. I didn't get to work with him again, which was sad for me in a way, as somehow I felt very close to him; he had worked with me purely to help his mum. He was a beautiful soul doing great work on the spiritual side of life. It gave me great comfort to know that when our loved ones take their own lives there are spirits like Stephen on the other side to help them move on.

I generally experience my guides as multidimensional beings; light is the best way I can think of describing them, light with a sense of humour, unlimited love and wisdom. I rarely see them, but I often sense them. I also call on Sai Baba, Christ and God for help at different times. It seems that, just as here, where we all have things we are good at or specialise in, so it is with the spiritual dimensions. For relationship issues I ask Archangel Michael for help and for the healing of animals I call on St Francis. If in doubt, ask for the highest and the best from within the light to help you.

# CHAPTER 9

# CONNECTING WITH YOUR HIGHER SELF

Eric was a successful businessman who sought me out before embarking on a business venture that involved considerable risk. The business opportunity would be very financially rewarding if it went well but, if it didn't, he would probably lose everything.

As a bank manager I would not have lent him money because there were too many variables outside of his control. But when I looked at him and the project he proposed clairvoyantly, a different picture emerged. I could see that he couldn't actually fail, because he was doing what he was doing for the right reasons — to satisfy a drive that came from deep within him, a heartfelt desire.

The opportunity here was one for growth; the lessons were in developing and extending his abilities and in trusting the higher power that was guiding him. I could see clairvoyantly that there were a couple of obstacles that were going to rear their heads — one to do with bureaucratic red tape — but they were nothing he couldn't get through.

It was clear that I had told Eric what he wanted to hear, and off he went. He phoned me a couple of times when the project hit a glitch and we talked things through, and then he was on his way again.

It was only some months later when he came to see me again that I realised I was not really being fair to Eric. Instead of telling him what I could see, I could have been teaching him how to access his own guidance. So at our next meeting, that is what I did. I took him through the following exercise and helped him to connect with his Higher Self so he could access his own inner knowing.

### EXERCISE: Connecting with your Higher Self
**Experience**

Ensure you will not be interrupted by phone calls or personal callers, and that you are dressed comfortably in loose-fitting clothes. When you are ready, start by sitting comfortably, with your spine erect. This is important to ensure a free flow of energy up and down your spine.

Close your eyes and take a few deep breaths. Really pay attention to your breathing — notice how it feels. Are you breathing from the top of your lungs or the bottom, or both? Don't try to change your breathing in any way, just notice it.

As you breathe, notice that you are also in a physical body. Notice how your physical body feels.

Feel your feet on the floor, feel the chair or ground beneath you, feel your fingers and your toes. Feel your shoulders, your neck ▶

and your head. Now feel yourself in the whole of your body at once and allow your body to relax.

Using your imagination, imagine that you can sense wise and loving spirit beings, forming a circle around you.

Using your imagination, imagine that you can see these wise and loving beings and that you see them as beings of light.

All around you now is a circle of wise and loving light beings standing just the right distance from you. Their presence helps you to feel safe and protected and loved. They want nothing from you. They are simply here to help you connect with your Higher Self.

Allow yourself to feel the love that these light beings are sending you. Feel their love for you gently opening your heart centre in the middle of your chest. You don't need to do anything, just allow yourself to feel the love and light they are sending you.

These light beings love you unconditionally. They know all that you have been through, all the choices you have made and why you made them, and they love you completely, exactly as you are.

Really let yourself feel the love they have for you and, as you do so, allow yourself to become aware of a brighter multidimensional light that is starting to approach the outside of the circle.

Allow yourself to feel the unconditional love and light that your Higher Self is sending to you. You might sense it as light, or as a feeling.

Notice how your Higher Self's higher and finer vibration is starting to merge with your own energy field, raising your own vibration. Notice how your own energy field is affected by this incoming stream of love and light.

Your Higher Self is approaching the circle perimeter now, and increasingly you can feel the love and light coming to you. Intend that your Higher Self connects with you. Feel yet more love and light streaming into your energy field, raising your vibration and your consciousness still further. Allow your Higher Self to merge with you fully. You and your Higher Self are becoming one.

Feel your Higher Self's love and wisdom as your energies intertwine. Allow yourself to sit as your Higher Self would sit. Notice your posture and your facial expression as you sit as your Higher Self. You and your Higher Self are as one.

As your Higher Self, reflect on your current life situation.

What is your life situation teaching you? (Pause)

What soul qualities are available to you, through your Higher Self, to help you in your current life situation? (Pause)

How can you get a better connection with your Higher Self? (Pause)

If you like, you can intend that your Higher Self stays with you now as you open your eyes.

The feeling of being larger than you physically are will gradually fade, but as you reflect on this experience you should still be able to access your Higher Self's wisdom for a time.

## Reflection

How did you feel? What did you learn? What did you think of the answers you obtained from your Higher Self? How long did the sensation last of being bigger than you physically are?

## Understanding

When you connect with your Higher Self you are connecting with an aspect of your own consciousness, an aspect of your soul that knows why you are here and what you are here to do.

I find connecting with my Higher Self very useful when I need to separate my life — who I basically am — from my life situation. If our life situation is bleak, say in the case of someone who has been diagnosed with terminal cancer, we can get really down unless we remind ourselves that we are not that cancer or that death sentence. We are, as we have always been, incredible beings having a physical experience.

Our Higher Self can often help us to see the bigger picture and separate the wood from the trees.

Our Higher Self can also be very useful in helping us to understand why we are here and what our life purpose is. There have been at least five billion people on Earth so far, and there are at least five billion people on Earth at this time. That makes you one in 10 billion.

You are not the way you are by chance; you have not had the life experiences you have by chance. There has never been another you in the whole of creation, and there never will again. You are beautifully, incredibly unique and you owe it to yourself to find out your life purpose.

Our life purposes tend to be multifaceted. On one level I could say that I am here to love and that I am here to learn, and this would probably be true for each of us. But we also have more individual life purposes. For example, my next book, *Conscious Living*, is a big part of what I am here to do. The book is already partly written and has been for some time, but I am not writing it. I am transcribing it, usually at 3.13 in the morning. I haven't brought the whole book through yet so I don't understand its full significance, but I do know at the core of my being that it is a profoundly significant book. And

I also know that the book is part of a much bigger whole.

I have an overview of the different projects I will be involved with and I also know some of the people I will be working with, but I don't get to see all of it, not till the time is right. Otherwise I might put the cart before the horse and mess things up. (Patience has been a big lesson for me this lifetime!) But I do know absolutely what my *next* steps are, and when the next step is to rest, or consolidate, or extend my boundaries or do nothing.

With this next exercise, the aim is to help you get a similar overview of your life purpose and to help you see and understand what the next steps are that you need to take.

## EXERCISE: Guided visualisation to discover your life purpose
### Experience

As always, ensure you will not be interrupted and that you are dressed comfortably. When you are ready, start by sitting comfortably, with your spine erect so that there is a free flow of energy up and down your spine.

Close your eyes and take a few deep breaths. Really pay attention to your breathing — notice how it feels. Are you breathing from the top of your lungs or the bottom, or both? Don't try to change your breathing in any way, just notice it.

As you breathe, notice that you are also in a physical body. Notice how your physical body feels.

Feel your feet on the floor, feel the chair or ground beneath you, feel your fingers and your toes. Feel your shoulders, your neck and your head. Now feel yourself in the whole of your body at once ❱

and allow your body to relax.

Imagine that you can sense wise and loving spirit beings, forming a circle around you.

Imagine that you can see these wise and loving beings with your internal vision and that you see them as beings of light.

All around you now are a circle of wise and loving light beings standing just the right distance from you. Their presence helps you to feel safe and protected and loved. They want nothing from you. They are simply here to help you connect with your Higher Self and to discover your life purpose.

Allow yourself to feel the love that these light beings are sending you. Feel their love for you gently opening your heart centre in the middle of your chest. You don't need to do anything, just allow yourself to feel the love and light they are sending you.

These light beings love you unconditionally. They know all that you have been through, all the choices you have made and why you made them, and they love you completely, exactly as you are.

Really let yourself feel the love they have for you and, as you do so, allow yourself to become aware of a brighter multidimensional light that is starting to approach the outside of the circle.

Allow yourself to feel the unconditional love and light that your Higher Self is sending to you. You might sense it as light, or as a feeling. Notice how your Higher Self's higher and finer vibration is starting to merge with your own energy field, raising your own vibration. Notice how your own energy field is affected by this incoming stream of love and light and know that the light contains information that is useful to you.

Your Higher Self is approaching the circle perimeter now, and increasingly you can feel the love and light coming to you. Intend that your Higher Self connects with you. Feel yet more love and light streaming into your energy field, raising your vibration and your consciousness still further. Allow your Higher Self to merge with you fully. You and your Higher Self are becoming one.

Feel your Higher Self's love and wisdom as your energies intertwine. Allow yourself to sit as your Higher Self would sit. Notice your posture and your facial expression as you sit as your Higher Self. You and your Higher Self are as one.

As your Higher Self, reflect on your life purpose. Intend to see and understand the different facets of your life purpose. Allow yourself to receive images, words and feelings about your life purpose.

How can you align your life situation with your life purpose? (Pause)

What are the next steps for you as far as your life purpose is concerned? (Pause)

What soul qualities are available to you, through your Higher Self, to help you in your life purpose? (Pause)

Allow your conscious mind to absorb all the information your Higher Self is sending and know that the detail of your life purpose will be revealed to your conscious mind in the perfect way at the pwerfect time. (Pause)

As you return to present-moment awareness, you can intend that your Higher Self stays with you as you open your eyes.

## Reflection

Take time to reflect on all that happened during this exercise. What did you see, sense, hear or intuit?

## Understanding

Some people find it easier to 'receive' information from their Higher Self than others. If you are sensing light but not words or pictures you may want to take this exercise one stage further.

As you sit as your Higher Self, think about your current work. As you think about your current work, does energy leave you or come into you? Is there more or less light?

Run different scenarios through your mind and notice what makes the energy stronger or weaker. For example:

*How does my Higher Self feel about working with plants?*
*How does my Higher Self feel about working with animals?*
*How does my Higher Self feel about working with people?*
*How does my Higher Self feel about working with the planet?*
*How does my Higher Self feel about working with the spirit world?*

Notice which causes the most invigorated enthusiastic feeling within you and then narrow the area down further. For example, if you had the strongest reaction to working with people try the following questions and notice which receives the most energised response:

*How does my Higher Self feel about working with children?*
*How does my Higher Self feel about working with youth?*
*How does my Higher Self feel about working with adults?*
*How does my Higher Self feel about working with the elderly?*
*How does my Higher Self feel about working with men?*
*How does my Higher Self feel about working with women?*
*How does my Higher Self feel about working with people who are out of work?*

By using a range of questions you should be able to identify the kind of work that would better align with your life purpose.

## Planning your next step

Don't expect to suddenly realise your whole life purpose overnight. Usually we are just shown the next few steps, but it is helpful to understand the general direction so we can make sure these steps are in alignment with the bigger picture.

Write down what you can about your life purpose at this stage and make a note in your diary to repeat this visualisation a week, two weeks and a month from now. One month from now compare what you know about your life purpose with the notes you have just made. If it is then clear that this visualisation is helping you to become more clear about your life purpose, revisit it on a monthly basis for the next six months or longer if you want to.

### Life's Purpose

To wonder at beauty,
Stand guard over truth,
Look up to the noble,
Resolve on the good:
This leadeth us truly,
To purpose in living,
To right in our doing,
To peace in our feeling,
To light in our thinking;
And teaches us trust,
In the working of Creation,
In all that there is,
In the width of the world,
In the depths of the soul. — RUDOLF STEINER

# CHAPTER 10

# MEDIUMSHIP

> Mediumship enables a beam of light to come through to the person's heart. It can give great joy to those on the physical and those in spirit.
>
> — FROM ONE OF MY OWN GUIDES

First you need to know that there are different levels within the spirit world. In the same way that the colours of the rainbow are on different frequencies, there are different frequencies within the spirit world.

## *The seven kingdoms/heavens*

To the best of my knowledge, at this time, this is my understanding of the spiritual dimensions.

We all originate from Godhead. We move away from Godhead to experience. In the first moving away from Godhead, we are not that far from Godhead. We still know ourselves as God and our frequency is very fine and very light. Our form, if I can call it that, is more like light than solid. We can move in any and all directions simultaneously, and we know ourselves as God.

We then move further away from Godhead to experience more, and we move into a slightly denser place, into the next heaven or kingdom. There are seven such planes or kingdoms, each one a little denser than the last, and for each plane we need a body of some kind. By the time we get here, to our physical presence on Earth, we have seven energy bodies, for the seven kingdoms, and a physical form, our body, which is the densest of all.

Many of us, at some time or another, have experienced a phenomenon known as astral travelling. Astral travelling is where your consciousness goes out of your body while you are asleep. You may have experienced yourself floating above your bed and seeing your sleeping body beneath you or, more commonly, feeling a lurch as your consciousness was suddenly pulled back into your body. This latter experience can feel rather unpleasant and is usually triggered by an unexpected noise disturbing sleep and causing the immediate return of your consciousness to your physical body.

When we die, we leave our physical body here and take our seven energy bodies with us. Where we go depends on our level of consciousness. Now, remember we are all equal. We all come from the same place — Godhead — and we all return there. We are all just at different stages in the journey; at different levels of consciousness.

If we have spent a life preoccupied with our own survival and with reproduction we will move into the first kingdom. It corresponds with the first or base chakra (*chakra* is a Sanskrit word meaning wheel; an energy centre in the body), and in that kingdom we operate through the energy body closest to our physical form. The first energy body can be very similar in appearance to our physical form. If you are sensitive you may be able to sense it about an inch away from your skin in this next exercise.

> ### EXERCISE: Sensing your aura
> **Experience**
> Clap and rub your hands together. Then close your eyes and bring your two palms slowly together. What do you sense? Warmth, resistance, breeze, a magnetic effect? You are learning to sense your own aura. If you don't feel anything initially, try repeating this exercise. Sometimes it takes a little while for our conscious brain to remember what this energy feels like.

The second kingdom is associated with the second or sacral chakra. If we have lived a life dominated by fear and pain, doing things to avoid pain/fear or to create fear/pain in others, we would move through into the second kingdom. We would operate in that kingdom using the second energy body a few inches away from the physical.

The third kingdom is associated with the third or solar-plexus chakra at the base of the breast-bone. If we have lived a life where we sought to control others, we would move through into the third kingdom.

The fourth kingdom is associated with the fourth or heart-centre chakra, on a line with the physical heart but more central. If we have lived a life where we learned to *feel* love, then we move through into this dimension. When I talk with the spirit world I usually make the link through this chakra.

The lower-frequency spirits cannot usually get through but I find all fourth centre and above can, so I open myself to all spirits who are able to *feel* love.

Spirits in the higher dimensions can visit the lower ones at will, simply by having that intent. So, if your grandmother was the salt of the earth, a lovely compassionate soul, she could visit another relative who perhaps didn't give so much love. In practice, it means that the more loving dimensions can influence the less loving, but not the other way around. It is a system that seems to work very well.

At any time we can choose to be more loving and progress through the kingdoms, or we can stay as we are because it is comfortable for us; because it is what we are used to. Just like on Earth really.

The fifth kingdom is the golden kingdom. It is associated with the throat chakra and is the one that most of us think of as heaven. In this dimension all our heartfelt desires are met; it is the one where we get whatever it is we want or dream of. To get there we have not only to be capable of feeling love, but we must also be able to express it in kind thoughts, kind words and kind actions. This kingdom has a lot of souls in it. It is so nice being there, souls are often so happy that they do not even wonder if there is anything else. But there is.

The sixth kingdom is where we go when we have learned to see God or good in everything, in every person and in every situation. It is associated with the third-eye chakra, in the middle of the forehead.

As far as I know, I came here to work on/demonstrate this one. My mother also taught me to do this from an early age.

I chose my mother — in fact, both parents — very well for the qualities and lessons they would give me.

Instinctively, you will know which kingdom you are working on too. If not, look at what is happening in your life right now or ask a close friend. They will usually be able to tell you. We often find it easier to recognise what someone else is working on.

Finally, the seventh kingdom. This is where go when we *know* ourselves as God, and it is associated with the crown chakra at the top of the head. Christ achieved this in his lifetime, demonstrated by his mastery over the physical; transforming water into wine; the feeding of the 5000; numerous healings and, ultimately, transcending his own physical body.

There have been other Masters too. Some are currently on the earth plane to assist humanity's awakening.

So when you work as a medium, having this knowledge about the different dimensions is extremely useful. If you want to communicate with the fourth kingdom — spirits who can feel love — you can automatically match their frequency by feeling love yourself. This is why, at all my shows I take time with the audience to get them feeling love. If there was too much lower vibration energy in the room, such as anger, fear or grief, I would not be able to work as well. If I opened up psychically in such an atmosphere I would only attract beings from the lower kingdoms and the whole experience would be quite traumatic for all concerned.

## Communicating with the spirit world

Communicating with the spirit world is much easier than most people think. Spirit beings are communicating with us much of the time; we just don't always pick up on what they are sending.

Communication is also becoming easier and easier, because of the higher energies coming into ourselves and the planet. Humanity's consciousness is rising and with it there is an incredible opportunity to access the spiritual realms. Once you know the mechanics of mediumship, how to open yourself to the correct frequency, then it is just a matter of listening for words, images, concepts and feelings, and getting lots and lots of practice.

For me, that meant practising on family and friends first of all and then joining a psychic fair to get more practice. When I first started communicating with spirit I was dreadfully slow.

One of the most moving consultations I did in my early days was for the father of a young man who had died in a car accident. Every piece of information I brought through took time. It was like pulling teeth. The young man in spirit was quite frustrated with me and wanted to get into my body and talk to his father through me, in his own voice. I was desperate to help but couldn't let go sufficiently to let the young man have control and, with hindsight, that was probably for the best. Fortunately his father, sitting in front of me, was a lot more patient than his son in the spirit world.

As soon as I opened up to the spirit world I could feel my feet on car pedals and a young man was showing me that he had been driving. He wanted me to tell his dad, the man sitting in front of me, that the accident had not been his fault.

'I have your son with me,' I explained. Dad nodded. 'He is

showing me him driving a car and asking me to tell you that the accident wasn't his fault.'

Dad shook his head. 'No, I can't accept that,' he said with a solemn face. There was no doubt in his mind that his son had been responsible for the accident.

I let my attention return to the son. This time I could see blood spurting down the left side of my body. I winced. 'Did your son injure his left side?' I asked, not knowing quite what to make of the images I was being shown.

'No,' Dad said, 'but I think I know what he's showing you.'

His response encouraged me to go on. I found myself drawing a cross, a Christian-style cross that was sufficiently large for me to write in. I found myself writing four names within the cross. It was a slow process but the young man's father was very patient with me.

In my mind's eye I saw a supermarket trolley and a loaf of bread. No sooner had these images disappeared than they were followed by a watch on a windowsill being picked up and put back down again. I told the father all that I had seen, and showed him all that I had written. I didn't understand the significance of the names I had written down inside the cross, and I didn't know if any of it would make sense to him.

I so desperately wanted to help both the father here and the son in spirit. I knew I had been very slow, and I apologised to the father before he had a chance to comment on what I had conveyed.

'I have not been doing this long,' I explained. 'I have to make sure each piece of information is correct before I pass it on. I know you desperately want proof. I am sorry if I haven't been able to give it. Please come and see me again when I have had some more experience.'

'That won't be necessary,' the father said. 'You are right. I did come here today wanting proof.' He took a moment to clear his throat. It was clearly very difficult for him even being with me and talking about his son. 'My son did die in a car accident, and he was driving. The four names you have written within the cross are the names of the four people who died in the car with him. The supermarket trolley and the loaf of bread make sense to me too. I was in the bakery section of a supermarket when I heard that my son had died.'

He took a moment or two to gather his emotions. 'The watch was his watch. I picked it up before coming here today and then I put it back down.'

I hadn't realised it but I had given him all the proof he needed. 'Why was there blood down the left side of his body?' I felt it was alright to enquire now as everything else had made sense and the father had said earlier that he thought he knew what that was. He explained that his son had ruptured the carotid artery in his neck on impact and would have been covered in blood.

My mediumship was better than I realised. I might be slow at times but I was certainly linking into the right level, and I realised for the first time that I was linking through my heart centre. I was holding my consciousness in the middle of my chest and hearing words and seeing images as I did this.

I learned through experience that if I hold my awareness in my heart centre, in the middle of my chest, I find my own spirit-world guides and also the loved ones of clients. Any lower and I can pick up people on the lower realms — troubled souls. Higher, and I connect with more loving, wiser beings.

It seems to me that our chakras are doorways through to the other dimensions. By holding our awareness there consciously we can communicate with the different dimensions at will. Now, if you are ready, it is time to put this theory to the test. When you first start communicating with the spirit world it is probably best to attempt communication for no more than 10 minutes at a time. You can do it more than once a day, but initially for no more than 10 minutes each session as this will enable you to keep your energy high and your attention focused.

### EXERCISE: Communicating with the spirit world

Do not attempt communication with the spirit world if you are emotionally upset or have taken either alcohol or drugs, as you may not have the level of control to make a safe and loving connection.

To communicate with the spirit world, sit comfortably, with your spine erect, and close your eyes. You may want to play relaxing music, burn incense or light a candle if this feels right for you. Remember that when communicating with the spirit world, *the secret is to not try too hard*. Remember this is a *natural* ability you have.

Start by noticing your breathing, what it is like to breathe. Remind yourself at a deep level that you are a living being. Then notice where your awareness is, and expand your awareness so that it senses the whole of your physical body at once. Remind yourself that you inhabit a physical body.

Now feel the part of you that is within; the part of you that has thoughts and feelings and a sense of humour. The part of you that has watched the seasons change and watched you grow older. Really let yourself become aware of the consciousness that inhabits your physical body. Notice how you can move this consciousness that you are out in front of your face, feeling the space in front of your face. Notice how you can expand your consciousness beyond your fingertips, feeling the space beyond your fingertips. Allow this to remind you at a deep level that your consciousness can transcend, or go beyond, the physical.

Now it is time to let your awareness rest in your heart centre, in the middle of your chest and on a line with your physical heart, but more central. Allow yourself to think loving thoughts about loved ones who have passed over, recalling happy memories, the good times you shared. Remember their laughter, their smile and how they made you feel.

After a few moments, ask if you have someone with you. You may feel a warm sensation, or a tingling, or your eyelids may start to flutter. Ask them to make the physical sensation stronger, so that you can be sure it is them and not your imagination.

Ask who it is. You may get a name or a face straight away. The image you see may be from a photo you remember — accept it. You may need to ask, 'Are you male?' and then 'Are you female?' and see which gets the stronger response.

What is their message for you? Is there anything they can tell you that you could not possibly know, that would prove that it really was them and not your imagination?

As you say 'goodbye', send your loved ones love and light and thank them for their help. Remember also to thank your guides. You may or may not have been aware of their presence but they will still be helping.

## Reflection

What happened? How do you feel about what happened? How was this different for you from communicating with your guide or your Higher Self?

## Understanding

People can get different results with this exercise. Don't be disheartened if not a lot seems to happen to begin with. The clearer you are that you want communication, and the more you allow yourself to sit and practise, the sooner you will start receiving communications.

*Remember: The secret of spirit-world communication is not to try too hard.*

As you become more experienced, you will be able to let the link continue for longer than a few minutes, and you will also be able to ask more meaningful questions. In time, you may want to try to bring someone through for someone else.

I have found that it is best if you know nothing about the other person, or at least nothing about their loved ones in the spirit world. That way you can more easily trust all that you 'receive' and check it out later to confirm that the link was sound and the information you received was correct.

The process of talking to the spirit world on behalf of another

MEDIUMSHIP

person is exactly the same as it is for yourself, except that you *intend* to communicate with a loved one for (name of person). You may want to hold a piece of jewellery belonging either to the person with you or the loved one who has passed over. I have found it works best to hold the jewellery in my left hand as this is the more sensitive side of the body, governed by the 'intuitive' right side of the brain. If you find the process is not working as well as you would like, take time to make sure the person you are with is relaxed. In relaxing them, you will also relax yourself.

A word of warning: When I first started receiving spirit communications for others, very often the first piece of information I was given was how the person had died. To make matters worse, I felt how they died in my own body. This was quite disconcerting to begin with. How a person passed over is useful evidence, but we don't need to feel what it is like to drown ourselves to prove there is life after death.

If you have this happen to you, tell the spirit politely but firmly 'Thank you. Tell me, rather than show me', or 'Not so strong please'. I often wonder if my experiences were so strong because I was such a sceptic and always wanted 'proof'. Perhaps they were as strong as they were because I was the one needing to be convinced, rather than the client!

So where to from here? Let spirit be your teacher. Don't be afraid to ask questions. If you don't get names initially, ask for them. If more than one spirit tries to communicate at one time tell them firmly they need to be one at a time or no one will be getting any messages through. Spirit can be remarkably co-operative. And if you want clients to practise on, just ask — spirit will bring them to you.

I believe that a great many people are capable of doing what I do and I now run workshops to help people develop their medium and clairvoyant abilities. For details, visit my website at *www.jeanettewilson.com*.

Your local Spiritualist Church or Spiritual Centre is also a good place to start. You can usually find them in the phone book. There you can speak with other like-minded people and perhaps join a developmental group.

Above all en-joy! Mediumship is something that brings great joy.

**Planning your next step**
What would be an appropriate next step for you as far as mediumship is concerned?

# PART 4

# DARE TO BELIEVE...
that you really can make a difference

# CHAPTER 11

# DARE TO BE YOU

In Part 1 of this book we looked at how you currently see the world, and how your map of reality may or may not be correct. We also identified that if a map is not accurate it will not help you get where you want to be, and that if you do not know that something is possible, such as spirit communication, you may not even attempt it.

In Part 2 we explored *how* we perceive our place in the world, using the *Logical Levels* model as a basis for our understanding. We saw how our beliefs affect our behaviour, which in turn shapes our experience of reality.

But our journey didn't end there, for no sooner had we identified the need to be familiar with our beliefs than we discovered the transient nature of these beliefs. We had to look elsewhere if we were to find out who we really were, and this meant going beyond our mind.

Part 3 took us into what, for some of us, are new territories, exploring meditation and different psychic phenomena.

Hopefully our experiences expanded our map of reality, and introduced us to new tools that we can use again and again to keep on pushing back our perception of ourselves, this reality and what is possible.

Part 4 is the shortest but most important part of the book. If it does not cause you to do something differently, then all of the preceding chapters will have been a waste of time. In this final part we pull together the threads of all that we have experienced and considered so far.

To do so we use exercises similar to those in Part 3 to help you to tap into *who* you really are, beyond mind.

First, we use a guided meditation to help you experience yourself without limitation or barriers. Then we call on your Higher Self and all the qualities of your Higher Self to help you bring this new awareness and understanding through into your consciousness, here and now.

In doing so you will find that any beliefs that no longer serve you will simply fall away. You will find your values realigning in a way that is truer to the real you, and you will find your behaviour changing in many practical and beneficial ways. You may get a new clarity about who you are and why you are here, and about the changes you need to make to align your life situation with your truth.

## EXERCISE: Guided meditation to experience yourself without limitation
### Experience

Allow yourself an uninterrupted period of 20 to 30 minutes to experience your self without limitation or barriers. Make sure that you will not be disturbed by phone calls or other interruptions. You may want to play some relaxing music or burn an aromatic oil to help you relax.

Sit or lie in a position that is comfortable for you. Let your awareness move down into your toes and, as you breathe out, imagine that you are breathing out all the tension stored in your toes. Just breathe it out and let it go. Allow your toes to relax more deeply than they ever have before. When your toes are completely relaxed, let your awareness move slowly into the rest of your feet.

Using your breath as a focus, imagine that you are breathing out all the tension stored in your feet. Just breathe it out and let it go. Allow your feet to relax more deeply than they ever have before. When your feet are completely relaxed, let your awareness move slowly into your ankles.

Notice how your ankles are feeling and, as you breathe out, imagine that you are breathing out all the tension stored in your ankles. Just breathe it out and let it go. Allow your ankles to relax more deeply than they ever have before. When your ankles are completely relaxed, completely at peace, let your awareness move into your lower legs.

Notice how this process of relaxing each part of the body in turn is already helping your lower legs to relax; it's as if they already know what to do. With every breath out the tension in your lower legs is releasing and dissolving. With each and every breath your ❯

lower legs are becoming more and more relaxed. Effortlessly now your awareness moves into your knees, and you notice that the tension that your knees are holding is already starting to release as with every breath out you breathe out tension. With each and every breath out you simply let go.

Even your upper legs are starting to relax now, as the feeling of relaxation spreads through your body. Every breath out releases tension from your upper legs; every breath out takes you into a deeper state of peace and relaxation. Allow your awareness to move gently and peacefully into your hips and pelvic area. You can feel the tension gradually releasing as with every breath out every cell learns to let go, letting go at a deeper level than they ever have done before.

It is as though each part of your body in turn is learning from the parts that have gone before and each part is becoming more relaxed as you gently and peacefully relax each part in turn. Soon the whole of your pelvic area is relaxed, more relaxed than it has ever been before.

You notice that the feeling of deep relaxation is making its way into your stomach and lower back. Every cell is giving up its tension to the out breath. Effortlessly and easily, every cell is becoming even more relaxed than it has ever been before.

And so the feeling of deep relaxation goes on, moving up into your chest and upper back. Every breath helps you release the tension; every breath helps you to feel even more relaxed. Even your shoulders are starting to soften now as the feeling of deep relaxation starts moving into them. Every breath is breathing out more tension; every breath is helping you feel more and more relaxed.

Allow yourself to breathe deeply now and really let your shoulders relax at a deep level. Every breath is breathing out tension; every breath is making you feel more relaxed and more at peace.

And as your shoulders allow themselves to relax completely, notice how that relaxed feeling is flowing down your arms and into your hands. With every breath you are breathing out tension stored in the arms and the hands; with every breath you are feeling more and more relaxed.

And that lovely relaxed feeling is flowing effortlessly into your neck and throat areas now. With every breath the cells of your neck and throat are feeling more relaxed, more at peace.

The feeling of deep relaxation is almost throughout your body now. So many parts of your body have allowed themselves to relax at a deep level that the remaining parts are already starting to do the same. You can feel your ears and eyes relaxing now, feel the muscles of your face relaxing.

It takes so much energy to hold on to tension but now you can simply breathe it out and let it go. Let all the tension that is stored in your head and face go. Allow all the cells of your body to relax at a deep level. Allow all your being to remember what it is to be relaxed and at peace.

You can't help but notice that every breath now is taking you deeper and deeper into a state of relaxation, deeper and deeper into the most peaceful state you have ever experienced. Every breath allows you to relax even more deeply, more deeply than you ever imagined possible. As you let yourself be completely relaxed, completely at peace, you realise that with every breath your sense of relaxation is becoming even more profound.

When you feel completely relaxed, notice how in this relaxed state it can feel almost as though your body has no outline. Gently let ▶

your awareness expand into the space around your body so you are feeling the space around you and your body at the same time. Once you have that sense of being bigger than you are physically, gently let your awareness expand further until you can feel yourself as large as a room. The more relaxed you become, the more your sense of awareness seems to expand, feeling yourself as large as a building.

Continue expanding your awareness until you can feel yourself the size of a street, a city, the planet, the universe, the 'All That Is'.

Feel yourself without boundaries or limitation now. Allow yourself to connect fully with the All That Is. Feel the love that is the All That Is. Realise that you can either allow this love and light to flow through you or you can block it by tensing and resisting. It is your choice. Notice how much less effort it takes to allow the love and light to flow through.

Notice how, if you have parts that are resisting, you can send them more love and light and help them to relax. Know that you are an important and integral part of All That Is. Allow yourself to feel this deep connection on all levels now.

Allow yourself to rest in this fully open and limitless state for as long as you feel the need. When you are ready, let your awareness start to come back to your physical body. Feel your awareness returning to your arms and your legs, and to your fingers and your toes. Soon you will be opening your eyes, but as you do so, realise at a deep level that this sense of connection and limitlessness has always been there for you, and will always be there.

Know that as you let your awareness return your cells will bring with them the memory and the knowledge of this limitless state and how it feels to be deeply connected to the All That Is. Know that at any time you will be able to access this limitless and fully connected state, simply by relaxing and having that clear intent.

### Reflection

What did you experience? How did you feel? Were there any insights for you doing this exercise?

### Understanding

This guided meditation helps you to use your mind to become aware of any blocks or barriers to your experiencing all that you are. It helps you locate any resistance that may not have been identified thus far on an energetic level.

Each time you do this exercise the feeling will be even more real and will affect you even more profoundly. It works simply because you hold the intent to feel yourself without boundaries or limitations.

To take this one stage further, do this next exercise soon after the last one. The next exercise is quite a powerful one and is ideally done with a friend, though you can do it by yourself if you wish. It takes about 30 minutes to complete.

You will need a large open space or a room free of obstacles because, for much of the exercise, you will have your eyes closed. You can start the exercise either seated or standing but be sure to have enough space in front of you to enable you to take four steps forward.

First, there is a guided visualisation to help you connect with your Higher Self. Then, when you can feel the presence of your Higher Self evidenced by feeling larger, bigger and lighter, you are going to imagine yourself walking from the centre of your *Logical Levels* outwards.

To do this you imagine a large version of the *Logical Levels* on the floor in front of you. It is large enough for you to step into comfortably and has clearly defined levels. When you are ready you will then be taking the new sense of who you are through into your beliefs and values and looking at them with new eyes, the eyes of your Higher Self.

You will find that some beliefs simply fall away, while others may arise within you for the first time. Then you will walk the new beliefs and values through into skills and capabilities, and look with new eyes at what skills and capabilities you have that align with your beliefs and values and at what new skills and capabilities you would like to acquire.

From there, you walk your skills and capabilities through into behaviours, and see yourself behaving as your Higher Self, noticing how you behave as your Higher Self, and particularly how you interact with others and what kind of work you do.

Finally, you walk your Higher Self through into your environment, noticing what is different about your environment and what needs to change.

### EXERCISE: Bringing your truth through

Make sure you are dressed comfortably, in loose-fitting clothes. When you are ready, start by sitting or standing comfortably, with your spine erect. This is important to ensure a free flow of energy up and down your spine.

Close your eyes and take a few deep breaths. Really pay attention to your breathing. Notice how it feels. Are you breathing from the top of your lungs or the bottom, or both? Don't try to change your breathing in any way, just notice it.

As you breathe, notice that you are also in a physical body. Notice how your physical body feels.

Feel your feet on the floor, feel the chair or ground beneath you. Feel your fingers and your toes, feel your shoulders, your neck and your head. Now, feel yourself in the whole of your body at once and allow your body to relax.

Using your imagination, imagine that you can sense wise and loving spirit beings, forming a circle around you. Imagine that you can see these wise and loving beings and that you see them as beings of light.

All around you now is a circle of wise and loving light beings, standing just the right distance from you. Their presence makes you feel safe and protected and loved. These loving light beings want nothing from you. They are simply here to help you connect with your Higher Self.

Allow yourself to feel the love that these light beings are sending you. Feel their love for you gently opening your heart centre in the middle of your chest. You don't need to do anything, just allow yourself to feel the love and light they are sending you.

These light beings love you unconditionally. They know all that you have been through, all the choices you have made, and why you made them, and they love you completely, exactly as you are.

Really let yourself feel the love they have for you and, as you do so, allow yourself to become aware of a brighter, magnificent, multidimensional light that is starting to approach the outside of the circle.

Allow yourself to feel the unconditional love and light that your Higher Self is sending to you. You might sense it as light, or as ❯

a feeling. Notice how your Higher Self's higher and finer vibration is starting to merge with your own energy field, raising your own vibration.

Notice how your own energy field is affected by this incoming stream of love and light. Your Higher Self is approaching the circle perimeter now, and increasingly you can feel the love and light coming to you. Intend that your Higher Self connects with you. Feel yet more love and light streaming into your energy field, raising your vibration and your consciousness still further.

Allow your Higher Self to merge with you fully. You and your Higher Self are becoming one. Feel your Higher Self's love and wisdom as your energies intertwine. Allow yourself to sit/stand as your Higher Self would sit/stand. Notice your posture and your facial expression as you sit/stand as your Higher Self. You and your Higher Self are now as one.

As your Higher Self imagine a large *Logical Levels* diagram on the floor beneath your feet. Imagine that you are standing in the centre two circles of the diagram — *Who?* and *Who else?* In front of you you can see the other levels clearly defined. *Why?* (values and beliefs), then *How?* (skills and capabilities), then *What?* (behaviours) and finally *Where?* and *When?* (environment).

Allow yourself to understand, at a deep level, in fact more deeply than ever before, who you are and who else exists. Feel yourself as your Higher Self in those centre two circles. Holding that feeling, when you are ready walk this new sense of who you are through into your beliefs and values and allow yourself to see them with new eyes, the eyes of your Higher Self.

Notice what happens to your beliefs. Do any change? Do any disappear? Do any new ones appear? Notice particularly what is different about seeing your beliefs and values through the eyes of your Higher Self.

Spend as long as you need on this level and then, when you are ready, maintain your Higher Self state and walk your new beliefs and values through into skills and capabilities. Look at your skills and capabilities with new eyes, the eyes of your Higher Self. What is different now? What has changed? As your Higher Self, what new skills and capabilities do you have? Again you can spend as long as you need on this level, noticing what is different.

When you are ready, maintaining your Higher Self state, walk your skills and capabilities through into behaviours. Notice the difference. What would you do differently as your Higher Self? What would you do more of as your Higher Self? What would you do less of as your Higher Self? What would you start doing? What would you stop doing? Notice how you would interact with others as your Higher Self, and notice the kind of work you would do as your Higher Self. Again, you can spend as long as you like at this level.

When you are ready, maintaining your Higher Self state, walk your behaviours through into the environment. What is different? What is the same? How are you spending your time? How is that different from before? What needs to change?

When you have seen all that you need to see, open your eyes. As your Higher Self, take time to note down your findings in as much detail as you can on a new *Logical Levels* diagram. What did you see? What did you hear? Were there any new insights or understandings? What was different for you?

While doing this exercise it is essential that the Higher Self state is maintained throughout. If the 'larger than life' feeling starts ❱

to fade, step back to the centre of the circles and connect once more with your Higher Self. Once the Higher Self state is stabilised within you, continue with the rest of the exercise.

### Reflection
How did you feel doing this exercise? What was the most striking realisation you had? Were you aware of any heartfelt desires? How do you feel now?

### Understanding
So why is this exercise so powerful? Most of us only rewrite our maps unconsciously when something happens to us. Most of the time we are not even aware of what has happened, or that we have changed our map.

In doing this exercise you are rewriting your map *consciously*, from the inside out, drawing on the highest aspect of consciousness that you have access to right now. In doing so you are accessing more of who you truly are, and bringing that through into reality. You are being more than you were before.

### Planning your next step
It is time to document the actions you would like to take to allow more of your Higher Self through.
- What do you need to do more of?
- What do you need to do less of?
- What changes do you need to make in your life situation to align it more fully with your truth?
- What do you need to stop doing? What do you need to start doing?

> If you can, break the changes down into smaller, more manageable little steps.
>
> Decide *when* you will make the changes and commit to taking the necessary action to allow more of the true you through. List what you will do today, tomorrow, next week, next month and so on. Diarise your actions.
>
> If you find it helpful, write key parts of your plan in large letters and post it on a wall. Tell others about what you will be doing.
>
> What support will you need internally? What support will you need externally? How will you get the support you need?
>
> How will you know when you have been successful? How may you sabotage your own plans? What contingency plans can you put in place to prevent this?

And so we have come full circle. We started by looking at the you that you were choosing to be at the beginning of this book, and we have ended by looking at the you you consciously choose to be now. It is time to compare the two.

## EXERCISE
Take out the *Logical Levels* diagram you completed when you started reading this book and compare it with the exercise you have just completed.

### Reflection
Notice what is different. How do you feel about the differences? ❯

Is there anything else you notice about the two diagrams that you were not aware of while you were walking through the levels?

## Understanding

The more we allow our awareness to be held in the centre of our being, the more conscious we become of who we truly are. The more we allow the light of our consciousness to shine in our lives, the clearer our way becomes. We find ourselves making better, more conscious choices for ourselves and our families.

We start to awaken to who we truly are and, in doing so, find the light within even more accessible. This is why, once you begin to awaken, start to become conscious, you cannot go back to your old way of being. You can't not be conscious again for any length of time once you have started to become conscious. Of course, you can still lose yourself from time to time with relationships and money and the world of form, but you can't ever go back to how you were before. Because now you are starting to real-ise (make real) your own truth, and the more you experience your own truth, the more you will want to experience it. There is no going back.

**Everything is shown up by being exposed to the light, and whatever is exposed to the light itself becomes light.**
— ST PAUL (EPH. 5:13)

As you take this new conscious you forward into your new future, remember not to underestimate the interconnectedness of all things. Everything you say, do, feel and think ripples out into the sea of consciousness that we are all part of.

## PRELUDE

Be conscious of your words, thoughts and actions, of the contribution you make to the whole and of the part you play. Everything you do makes a difference. It did before; it's just that you were not so conscious of it then.

This stage in humanity's evolution is a particularly exciting one, for not everyone is conscious *yet*. So those who are conscious have a much greater effect on the future we create for ourselves than those who lack consciousness. That gives me great hope.

May the future you are presently creating be rooted in love, and guided by your highest truth. For you are the light of the world!